S.S.F. Public Library
West Orange
840 West Orange Ave.
South San Francisco, CA 94080

SSF

S.S.F. Public Library
West Orange
840 West Orange Ave.
South San Francisco, CA 94080

FEB   2005

CULTURES OF THE WORLD®

PAKISTAN

Sean Sheehan & Shahrezad Samiuddin

BENCHMARK BOOKS

MARSHALL CAVENDISH
NEW YORK

S.S.F. PUBLIC LIBRARY
WEST ORANGE AVENUE

PICTURE CREDITS
Cover photo: © Mike Zens/CORBIS
AFP: 44, 121 • R. L'Anson: 13, 80, 94, 125, 126 • APA: 3, 4, 49, 54, 75, 85, 118, 128 • Bushra J. Butt: 130
• CORBIS: 14, 28, 39, 42, 47 • Eye Ubiquitous: 8, 89, 104 • Hans Hayden: 6, 40, 122 • Hulton-Deutsch:
24, 25 • Hutchison Library: 5, 7, 31, 45, 55, 59, 83, 87, 92, 98, 119 • Image Bank: 90, 93 • B. Klingwall:
17, 21, 60, 82, 86, 91, 111 • Life File: 12, 50, 57, 63, 66, 70, 71, 74, 99, 105, 106 • Lonely Planet Images:
41, 131 • Christine Osborne: 10, 11, 15, 19, 20, 22, 30, 33, 34, 35, 36, 38, 52, 53, 62, 64, 65, 67, 69, 73,
76, 77, 78, 79, 88, 95, 97, 100, 101, 107, 110, 116, 117, 120, 124, 127 • Pakistan High Commission,
Singapore: 23, 29 • Pakistan International Airlines: 61 • Peter Sanders Photography: 103 • Bernard
Sonneville: 112, 115 • Sunday Times, Singapore: 109 • Audrius Tomonis: 135 • Travel Ink: 1, 58
• Nik Wheeler: 16, 26, 32, 72, 84, 114 • Alison Wright: 48

ACKNOWLEDGMENTS
Thanks to Philip Oldenberg of the Southern Asian Institute at Columbia University for his expert
reading of this manuscript.

PRECEDING PAGE
The wide smile of a young Pakistani in Karakoram shines with the colors of her traditional outfit.

Marshall Cavendish
99 White Plains Road
Tarrytown, NY 10591
Website: www.marshallcavendish.com

© Times Media Private Limited 1996, 1994
© Marshall Cavendish International (Asia) Private Limited 2004
All rights reserved. First edition 1994. Second edition 2004.

® "Cultures of the World" is a registered trademark of Marshall Cavendish Corporation.

Originated and designed by
Times Books International, an imprint of
Marshall Cavendish International (Asia) Private Limited,
a member of the Times Publishing Group

All rights reserved. No part of this book may be reproduced or utilized in any form or
by any means electronic or mechanical, including photocopying, recording, or by an
information storage and retrieval system, without permission from the copyright owner.

Library of Congress Cataloging-in-Publication Data
Sheehan, Sean, 1951-
Pakistan / by Sean Sheehan. — 2nd ed.
    p. cm. — (Cultures of the world)
Includes bibliographical references and index.
    ISBN 0-7614-1787-7
1. Pakistan—Juvenile literature. I. Title. II. Series.
DS376.9.S49 2004
954.91—dc22   2004007677

Printed in China

7 6 5 4 3 2 1

CONTENTS

A rural Hunza man.

Two Kalash girls.

INTRODUCTION

MANY OF THE CATCHPHRASES that have become clichés in travel brochures are lived out in Pakistan. The country and its people are diverse, a potpourri of cultures. Nomadic ethnic groups in Sind still collect roots and berries, while hill Pashtuns carry guns and knives and observe a code of honor for their use that would have impressed medieval knights or heroes of the American Wild West. At the same time, Lahore churns out movies regularly.

Despite the exotic diversity, Pakistan is unified by religion. Born of a need for Muslims in India to have a country of their own, Pakistan came into existence in 1947 amid one of the bloodiest conflicts of the 20th century. Its political situation since then has continued to be full of conflict, with elected leaders being deposed every few years.

Pakistan has been called "a castle with a thousand doors," and this book sets out to open some of these doors. Its history, geography, languages, lifestyles, habits of dress and thought, and much else are dealt with in words and pictures that bring to life a fascinating country.

GEOGRAPHY

PAKISTAN IS A COUNTRY in the northwest of the Indian subcontinent. To the east and southeast is India, to the west is Iran, to the northwest is Afghanistan, and to the north is China. Mountains extend from the north to the Arabian Sea and at their base is the broad valley of the Indus river. There are four provinces: Punjab, Sind, Baluchistan, and North-West Frontier. Five tributaries of the mighty Indus water the plateau of Punjab, the area of Pakistan most blessed by nature. Other regions of the country, Baluchistan for example, are different in character and impose harsher conditions on the people who live there. The regional differences in landscape and fertility of the soil mirror the differences of the peoples who live off the land.

Opposite: **A tributary of the Indus River runs through rice fields in Pakistan.**

Below: **Terraced hills, which maximize agricultural use of the land, are a common sight.**

Part of the Hindu Kush mountain range in Baluchistan. The name of the range means Mountains of India in Arabic.

MOUNTAINS

Three great mountain ranges dominate Pakistan: the Himalayas, the Karakoram Range, and the Hindu Kush. The Himalayas form the highest mountain system in the world.

The Karakoram Range stretches for about 300 miles (480 km) and contains 60 peaks that rise over 22,000 feet (6,700 m). Most of Pakistan's highest mountains are part of the Karakorams and are found within the disputed Kashmir border with India.

The Hindu Kush mountain range stretches for about 500 miles (800 km) along Pakistan's border with Afghanistan. Most of these mountains are permanently covered with snow. This is the location of the famous Khyber Pass, which links Peshawar in Pakistan and Kabul in Afghanistan. It has been used as an entrance by armies invading the Indian subcontinent.

Mountaineers are fascinated by the challenge of scaling the high peaks of these three ranges, and Pakistanis participate in many climbing expeditions. Some are porters, carrying supplies to base camps from where the real climbing begins; others are professional mountaineers. They accompany the climbers and provide invaluable information and assistance in coping with the rigors of the high-altitude environment. During the winter months, the snow freezes into a slippery, icy mass, making climbing impossible. It is only in mid-April that the climbing season gets under way. It may be spring, but the temperature remains below freezing above 2,000 feet (609 m) so there is a danger of frostbite even with the sun shining brightly overhead.

THE CHALLENGE OF K2

Rising in splendid isolation at the head of the Baltoro Glacier, K2 is the second highest mountain peak in the world. At 28,251 feet (8,611 m), it is only 784 feet (239 m) lower than Mount Everest.

K2 was discovered in 1856 by Colonel T.G. Montgomerie, a Survey of India employee. It was previously called Godwin Austen, after the English geologist who first surveyed the mountain, but this name was never officially recognized. The mountain was named K2 because it was the second to be measured in the Karakoram Range.

K2 is considered by most professional mountaineers to be far more difficult to climb than Everest, and many consider it virtually unscalable. A group of English and Swiss climbers first attempted to climb K2 in 1902. This was followed by other expeditions in 1909, 1938, 1939, and 1953 by various European and American teams. All failed to reach the summit, and these efforts resulted in several deaths.

Despite the dangers, an Italian team led by Ardito Desio, a geologist, conquered K2 on August 31, 1954. This success, however, was marred by the death of one of the climbing guides. In 1986 nine expeditions converged on the mountain, and 27 climbers, including the first woman, reached the summit. However, success was accompanied by tragedy; 13 people of various nationalities died between June and August that year on K2.

The fertile Indus Valley has made the provinces of Punjab and Sind the breadbasket of Pakistan.

THE INDUS VALLEY

The Indus Valley is a vast region of some 200,000 square miles (518,000 sq km) and constitutes the most prosperous agricultural region of Pakistan. The province of Punjab is in the northern part of this area. The literal meaning of Punjab is five waters, referring to the five important tributaries of the Indus that flow through Punjab and provide an invaluable supply of water. One of these tributaries lies within India's borders. The greatest population density is found in Punjab, and Islamabad, the nation's capital, lies in the northern part of this region.

The areas between rivers are known as *doab* (DOH-aab). Improved irrigation techniques have turned these areas into rich agricultural land. Pakistan has the most extensive man-made irrigation system in the world. The irrigation, however, is causing problems in the form of waterlogged soil and excessive salinity. The rate of evaporation is greater than the rate of rainfall, and therefore mineral salts accumulate in the water. As the salts

THE INDUS

With a drainage area of 450,000 square miles (1,165,500 sq km), 60 percent of which lies in Pakistan, the Indus is indisputably the great waterway of the country. The river is one of the longest in the world; its journey of 1,800 miles (2,900 km) begins in Tibet, where it starts as little more than melting ice from the glaciers of the Himalayas. It is also one of the most powerful rivers in the world, with an annual flow that is twice that of the Nile.

Each summer, the sun melts so much ice that the river overflows its banks as it winds its way south. The rich alluvial plains of the provinces of Punjab and Sind are largely formed by the fertile silt deposited by the Indus and its tributaries.

Farther south, the river enters a narrow gorge. It is here that it can most easily be harnessed for irrigation. Indeed, so much water is removed from the Indus for irrigation that big boats can no longer use the river, although small boats can navigate the final stage of the river's journey to the Arabian Sea during the monsoon season from July to September.

With the help of modern technology, Pakistan is exploiting the river's value as a source of power and irrigation. Large dams have been constructed to hold back the summer floods and release the waters later into the numerous irrigation canals that dot the landscape of Punjab and Sind. The two main dams are the Mangla and the Tarbela. Hydroelectric plants have also been constructed along the river in order to provide electricity for the industrial centers and towns of the Indus Valley.

find their way into the land, they slow down plant growth and increase the likelihood of the soil becoming infertile. The problem of salinity is more severe in Sind than in any other region of the country. Pakistan's scientists are working on ways to neutralize the salinity; they are also working on developing a hardy wheat hybrid that will thrive in saline soil.

The four tributaries join the Indus in east-central Pakistan.

BALUCHISTAN

This large province in west and southwest Pakistan occupies an area of over 134,050 square miles (347,188 sq km). It is separated from the Indus Valley by mountains and is generally a high and rocky area averaging over 1,000 feet (305 m) in elevation. Despite this inhospitable geography, the Baluchis manage to survive using a unique system of irrigation known as the *karez* (kah-REZ). At the foot of the rocky hills, water is collected in underground canals and carried to neighboring fields where it is drawn off into strategically located well shafts. The underground canals minimize water loss through evaporation. Farmers manage to grow some crops and supplement this by rearing sheep and goats.

The hardy Baluchis valiantly try to eke out a living from their inhospitable land.

CLIMATE

The amount of rainfall in Pakistan varies not only from region to region, but also from year to year. The word monsoon originally described a wind over the Arabian Sea, but is now used to describe the rainy seasons of east Asia and Africa. Pakistan's vast land mass warms up during the summer, and, as the air warms and rises, the air pressure is reduced. Warm, moist air from the oceans is then drawn inland by the seasonal wind. Thus it rains mostly from June to September. Eastern Punjab receives 20 inches (51 cm) of rain a year, while most of Baluchistan receives less than five inches (13 cm) a year. The heaviest rains fall near the high mountains in the north. Annual rainfall here can be as much as 35 inches (89 cm) a year.

Hot, rainy summers and long, cold winters are the norm. In the north, summer temperatures average 75°F (24°C) and in the winter freezing temperatures are common. In Punjab and Sind, summer temperatures average 93°F (34°C), falling to 55°F (13°C) in winter. Baluchistan experiences similar temperatures that are generally lower than those of Punjab.

The faster the warm, moist air is forced to rise, the shorter and heavier the rain showers become. Not surprisingly, then, the mountainous region in the north of the country experiences the highest rainfall.

FLORA AND FAUNA

The most exciting wildlife is found in the North-West Frontier Province, where bears and leopards still roam. This is where the increasingly rare snow leopard—also known as the clouded leopard because its thick, pale gray, dark-ringed coat resembles clouds—can still be found living in the forests near the snow line. The clouded leopard is a protected species as only about 250 remain. Its numbers decreased rapidly in the 20th century due to hunting and deforestation.

Another protected species is the bustard. The bustard, a large fowl and a popular food source, has been excessively hunted and is now in danger of extinction. With the help of the World Wildlife Fund, the government is working to preserve the species.

Around the southern delta, crocodiles and pythons are common. Also found here is the Indus river dolphin, which is blind and navigates by sonar. It is also a protected species.

The dry climate and the hot summers determine the plant life to a large extent. Apart from plantations and orchards, trees are not common; low-lying bushes are more likely to be seen in the landscape. Typical vegetation consists of short grass, and in Baluchistan only xerophytic plants—plants adapted to hot, dry climates—are likely to survive.

The Thar Desert (also known as the Great Indian Desert) covers part of eastern Pakistan and, although it contains patches of clay among the tracts of pure sand, there is virtually no vegetation.

The snow leopard lives in the mountains of central Asia and the Indian subcontinent. It hunts at night and preys on different kinds of animals.

CITIES

The majority of Pakistanis live in the countryside, but there are half a dozen cities with populations exceeding 500,000. Islamabad is the capital, but the city with the largest population is Karachi, where approximately 10 million people live. Karachi, situated on the coast of the Arabian Sea, became Pakistan's capital in 1947. However, Karachi was regarded as an inconvenient center for the federal government, and a commission was set up in 1959 to choose a site for a new city. Construction began two years later, and in 1966 the first office building in Islamabad was occupied.

Unlike most cities in Asia, which mushroomed haphazardly around rivers or deltas, the site for Islamabad was selected by a committee and development was planned in an orderly fashion.

Islamabad is not like any other city in Pakistan. Having been planned from scratch, it exhibits little of the haphazard development that characterizes many Asian cities. In addition, more than six million trees have been planted to provide the city with pleasant greenery.

Islamabad offers a complete contrast to Rawalpindi, a neighboring city about 9 miles (14 km) to the southwest, which was founded in the 14th century by a local ethnic group and developed by the British in the 19th century. Rawalpindi is a noisy, bustling place, typical of Pakistan's urban centers, and the city's bazaars attract traders from neighboring Kashmir and beyond. A busy highway connects Islamabad and Rawalpindi, also known as just 'Pindi. The two cities have become a massive twin-city metropolis sharing urban services and amenities.

HISTORY

THE HISTORY OF PAKISTAN unfolds into a dramatic sweep of events that features some of the world's greatest empires. Persians, Greeks, Turks, Mughals, and the British have all fought over the land, established their cultures, and then faded away as new forces made their presence felt.

Yet the country where these civilizations flourished and then floundered did not come into existence as a separate nation until 1947. Until then, the country known today as Pakistan was part of India. The years since the Partition in 1947 have been equally eventful and turbulent, and, perhaps, even more intriguing.

Opposite: **The massive Lahore Fort was built by Mughal emperor Akbar between 1586 and 1618 to defend Lahore, a city of strategic importance for the Mughal empire.**

Below: **A view of the main bath at Mohenjo Daro, a civilization that flourished along the Indus River 4,500 years ago.**

THE INDUS VALLEY CIVILIZATION

Archaeologists began to unearth evidence of this great civilization during the 1920s. Digging began around two town sites—Mohenjo Daro near the Indus River and Harappa in Punjab province—and revealed a culture that extended some 1,000 miles (1,600 km) from the Himalayan foothills to the Arabian Sea. It is sometimes referred to as the Harappan civilization.

The Indus Valley civilization flourished about 4,500 years ago, although its origins remain unclear. Historians speculate that nomadic tribes settled along the river plain, perhaps imitating the successful agriculture begun by earlier, more dispersed farming communities. Undoubtedly, the cycle of the Indus was crucial, for as the water receded each summer, the alluvial soil left behind provided rich earth for agriculture without the need for plowing or manuring. How this farming lifestyle evolved into a mature and sophisticated culture remains a mystery. While there is some evidence suggesting that force was employed, it is also likely that the period of development was a slow and mainly peaceful process.

Tangible evidence provides proof of an impressive society. Animals were domesticated, crops harvested and stored in warehouses, copper mined, and city streets laid out on a grid pattern. Houses were constructed of bricks, and unlike other early civilizations, such as the Nile Valley civilization in Egypt, the extent of urban planning suggests that houses were not just for the privileged few but were, in fact, inhabited by the bulk of the population.

An extensive drainage system for sanitation and the use of a uniform system of weights and measures

Many engraved seals made of soapstone, like this one found at Harappa, depict bulls and have formal pictorial symbols written from right to left.

support the idea that a central authority planned and coordinated matters of public interest.

The communities of the Indus Valley did not live in complete isolation. Trade was conducted with south India, Afghanistan, Arabia, and Central Asia, and there is evidence to suggest that sea trade facilitated the exchange of goods and raw materials with Mesopotamia, another great civilization then developing between the Euphrates and Tigris rivers in the Middle East.

This highly developed urban civilization eventually began to stagnate and went through a state of decline due to natural catastrophes, such as floods and overpopulation. Mohenjo Daro's abrupt end occurred in the second millennium B.C. Scholars have proposed that this was due to attacks by invading forces, thought to be Aryans. Towns were abandoned and the people probably returned to a nomadic way of life. An inspiring experiment in urban planning, a settled agriculture, and a peaceful existence thus came to an end.

While excavations are continuing to reveal the immense complexity and sophistication of the Indus Valley civilization, there are still many unanswered questions.

This bridge of boats spanning the mighty Indus River is the only mark Alexander the Great left on Pakistan.

THE ARYANS AND AFTER

From Persia, the Aryans arrived in what is now Pakistan around 2000 B.C. Little archeological evidence of their presence remains, although their written scripts, which make up the Vedas, are important sources for studying the origin of the Indian caste system and Hindu religious beliefs.

Alexander the Great crossed the Hindu Kush twice, once in 329 B.C. via Khawak Pass and later in 327 B.C. via Bamian. After that his battle-weary troops were not inclined to travel farther east, so he sailed down to the Indus delta and from there returned to Babylon in 323 B.C. He died the same year.

In the centuries that followed, many peoples from different parts of Asia ruled what is now Pakistan: the Indians from the Maurya Empire, the Greeks of Bactria, the Huns, the Arab Muslims, and the Ottoman Turks, followed much later by the mighty Mughals.

THE MUGHAL EMPIRE

By the early 16th century, the Mughals, with an army of elephants and muskets with matchlocks, had established control over northern India and what is now Pakistan. The first Mughal emperor was Babur (1483–1530), whose military genius initiated some 200 years of Mughal rule. He was a descendant of Timur (Tamerlane) and Genghis Khan. Babur possessed a love of learning and was an enlightened ruler. His son Humayun (1508–1556) lacked the energy and vision of his father but was responsible for introducing aspects of Persian art and the Persian language into the Mughal domain. The culture of Pakistan was significantly affected by the Mughals.

The next Mughal emperor was Akbar (1542–1605). Generally considered the greatest of the Mughals, Akbar ruled for nearly 50 years. The Mughal empire was firmly established during this time, and after 1585 Akbar moved his capital from near Agra in India to Lahore, now in Pakistan, where he built the magnificent Lahore Fort.

Akbar was succeeded by Jahangir (1569–1627), famous for his encouragement of the arts and equally infamous for his addiction to drugs and alcohol. After his death, his son Shah Jahan (1592–1666) became emperor and has been immortalized as the mastermind behind the building of the Taj Mahal in India. Shah Jahan died in his Agra palace. He was imprisoned there by his son Aurangzeb (1618–1707), who was the last great Mughal emperor.

Shah Jahan built the Taj Mahal in memory of his beloved wife Mumtaz Mahal, and is buried there beside her.

PAKISTAN AND THE BRITISH

Soon after Vasco da Gama discovered a sea route to India in 1498, European traders began to make their presence felt in Asia. The East India Company was founded by British merchants in 1600 and, over the next two and a half centuries, the company gradually extended its control through military and political means. By the time the company was disbanded in 1858, Punjab and Sind had become part of British India, the jewel in the crown of the British Empire.

The British badges carved into the rocks near the Khyber Pass are a reminder that the British Empire once extended to this part of the world.

The North-West Frontier Province and Baluchistan were highly valued as buffer states against Russia and, by the beginning of the 20th century, the whole of what is now Pakistan was part of British India.

Many historians attribute the creation of Pakistan to the policies of the British in India. The spread of Western education, in particular, had the effect of alienating Muslims, who were more inclined to insist on their own religious schools than were the Hindus. At the same time, the British were willing to exploit the religious differences in order to weaken the threat posed by the Indians' demand for self-government.

By the end of World War II, independence for India was inevitable, but the British thought that an independent Muslim state was also inevitable, as Muslims refused to live under a majority Hindu-ruled India. In 1946 thousands of people died during religious conflicts in Calcutta. The pressure for a new Muslim state was spearheaded by Muhammad Ali Jinnah, a man whose name is inseparable from the birth of Pakistan.

MUHAMMAD ALI JINNAH (1875–1948)

When Muhammad Ali Jinnah joined the Indian National Congress as a young man, the Congress represented both Hindu and Muslim hopes for self-determination.

At first Jinnah was an ardent supporter of Hindu-Muslim unity and was even termed the best ambassador of this ideology for his efforts. However, he became disillusioned with Mohandas Gandhi's leadership of the Congress. Division among his fellow Muslims eventually served to expel him from leadership of the Punjab Muslim League and, in 1930, he left for England. By the time he returned in 1935, he had abandoned the idea of Hindu-Muslim unity and was stridently advocating a separate home for India's Muslims.

Jinnah campaigned for an independent Pakistan, which means "the land of the pure" in Urdu. The big problem was how to determine which parts of India would become Pakistan.

When Jinnah's Pakistan emerged in 1947, it was unique, consisting of two parts separated by 1,000 miles (1,609 km) of Indian territory. In the northwest, the provinces of Sind, Punjab, North-West Frontier, and Baluchistan became West Pakistan, and in the northeast, Bengal became East Pakistan. The Bengalis shared the Muslim religion with the West Pakistanis, and were ardent supporters of Pakistan.

Jinnah was the first governor-general of the new country and president of its Assembly, but his time as Pakistan's leader was short-lived. He died on September 11, 1948.

CIVIL WAR

Pakistan was created with bloodshed and conflict. Its birth resulted in the world's largest mass movement of people. Some 7.5 million Muslims from India fled to the two parts of Pakistan, and about 10 million Hindus left Pakistan for the new India. Muslims stopped trains carrying Hindus out of Pakistan and murdered the passengers, and there were similar attacks by Hindus on Muslims fleeing India.

In 1956 a new constitution declared Pakistan an Islamic republic, but there was always an undercurrent of tension between West and East Pakistan. This tension was one of the factors that convinced military leaders they could run the country better than the politicians, and in 1958 the military abolished the constitution and took control. A new constitution was drawn up in 1962.

The partition of India and Pakistan resulted in the deaths of over one million people as Hindus and Muslims murdered each other.

ELECTIONS By 1970, the military had organized elections and seemed prepared to return government to an elected assembly, but events were soon to lead to civil war.

When a cyclone and tidal wave struck East Pakistan in 1970 many Bengalis were convinced that the government in West Pakistan allowed long delays in organizing their relief. Then, because of East Pakistan's numerical superiority, the elections organized by the military resulted in a majority of seats in the new Assembly going to Bengalis. East Pakistan demanded autonomy in all areas of government except foreign policy. When West Pakistan refused to entertain these

Zulfikar Ali Bhutto, Pakistan's leader from 1971 to 1977, was a progressive leader, implementing major reforms to alleviate the plight of the poor.

demands, East Pakistan declared itself an independent nation called Bangladesh in March 1971. West Pakistan then sent the army to bring Bangladesh under control. In December 1971, India sided with Bangladesh and went to war against Pakistan. Pakistan was defeated within two weeks, and the war came to an end at the cost of one million lives. Pakistan had lost half its population and a seventh of its area. Yahya Khan, the president of Pakistan, resigned.

BHUTTO AND GENERAL ZIA

Zulfikar Ali Bhutto was appointed to be the president of Pakistan from 1971 to 1973 and later became its prime minister from 1973 to 1977. He introduced a new constitution in 1973 based on adult suffrage. When Bhutto called for elections in 1977, widespread allegations of vote-rigging were made and civil disorder erupted across the country. On July 5, 1977, Bhutto was placed under house arrest by General Muhammad Zia ul-Haq, who accused Bhutto of having ordered the murder of a political rival. Bhutto was found guilty and sentenced to death by hanging. He was executed in 1979. General Zia had promised new free elections, but he was still ruling the country when he died in a plane crash in 1988.

A modified version of the 1973 constitution was introduced in 1985, and elections were held under restricted conditions. As a result, they were boycotted by the main opposition groups. The elections in 1988 were a different matter, and Benazir Bhutto, the daughter of the executed Bhutto, was elected the new prime minister. Benazir Bhutto, the first woman to become prime minister of an Islamic country, did not have the support of the military and in 1990 she was deposed. New elections were held, but it is believed that they were rigged to bring to power someone acceptable to the army. That person was Nawaz Sharif. He alienated the army and the president, however, and was deposed by the president in April 1993. A month later, the Supreme Court ruled the ouster illegal, and Nawaz Sharif was reinstated only to be forced to resign in July. A general election was scheduled for October. Although Benazir Bhutto's party did not win a majority, she was elected to head a coalition government, and she returned to power. She was again dismissed on charges of corruption in 1996.

Nawaz Sharif won the elections in 1997 and became the prime minister again. Two years later, he was replaced by General Pervez Musharraf after a bloodless military coup. Musharraf declared himself president in 2001.

General Zia ruled Pakistan with an iron fist, and all political opposition was firmly and often violently suppressed. Because Pakistan opposed the Soviet Union's invasion of Afghanistan, international disapproval of Zia's regime was muted by U.S. support for him.

GOVERNMENT

GIVEN PAKISTAN'S TURBULENT HISTORY, it is not surprising that there have been many changes of government. The army has often been a key player in the process of governing the country, and high-ranking members of the armed forces, usually with the support of business interests, have intervened repeatedly in the government by deposing existing administrations. Nevertheless, a democratic tradition remains, despite the likelihood of vote-rigging and unconstitutional changes enforced by those who gain power.

THE CONSTITUTION

There are two main parties in Pakistan, the Pakistan People's Party led by Benazir Bhutto, and the Pakistan Muslim League led by Nawaz Sharif. Both individuals are Pakistan's former prime ministers.

After East Pakistan became Bangladesh in 1971, it was necessary to reorganize the administration to adapt to the new situation. The smaller provinces feared domination by the Punjab, where over 60 percent of the population lives. Zulfikar Ali Bhutto introduced a constitution that balanced power between a national assembly elected by the whole country and regional assemblies based in Sind, Punjab, Baluchistan, and North-West Frontier provinces. Consensus was achieved, and the constitution was formally adopted in 1973. The present Pakistani Constitution is a less democratic version of the 1973 constitution.

The most notably undemocratic feature of the present constitution arises from an amendment introduced by General Zia in 1985 and again by General Pervez Musharraf in 2002. The amendments give the president of the country the right to overrule the elected assembly. Pakistan's current president is also its army chief, General Musharraf.

The 1973 Constitution is the third in Pakistan's history and is likely to remain the basis of any future democracy in the country.

Opposite: **A policeman guards the Khyber Pass, which is the traditional route for invasions into the Indian subcontinent from Central Asia.**

In October 1999 the government experienced some upheaval. Prime Minister Sharif was removed in a military coup and exiled to Saudi Arabia. General Musharraf then proceeded to reinvent the country's political system by making drastic changes to the constitution. An elected parliament came into being as a result of the elections held in October 2002. The prime minister has little authority; the real power of governance rests with the president, who is also the army chief.

BENAZIR BHUTTO

In December 1988 Benazir Bhutto, at 35, became the first woman premier of a modern Islamic state. She was deposed in 1990 but returned to power as prime minister from 1993 to 1996. She remains enormously popular today, especially among the millions of poor peasants who make up the majority of Pakistan's population.

Her upbringing was a privileged one, as she was born into one of the richest families in Pakistan. She was educated at a series of private English schools in Pakistan, and at the age of 16 went to the United States to study at Harvard-Radcliffe University. She then continued her studies at Oxford University in the United Kingdom.

When she returned to Pakistan in 1977, she was expecting to enter the foreign service of a government ruled by her father, Zulfikar Ali Bhutto. But within a week of her return, her father was overthrown by the army, and he was hanged two years later. Benazir Bhutto recalls seeing him for the last time: "The last time I saw him was a few hours before his

As president of Pakistan, General Pervez Musharraf has the power to overrule and dismiss the elected Assembly, a power he threatens to exercise when opposition parties demand greater power from parliament.

assassination on April 3. He weighed 95 pounds at the time. It was terrible and extremely traumatic. It's a very painful chapter and I don't know how one ever comes to terms with it."

In her first term, Bhutto was prime minister of Pakistan for two years before being dismissed on charges of corruption in 1990. In 1991, her husband, labeled a polo-playing millionaire by the press, was arrested and also charged with corruption. Bhutto supported her husband's claim of innocence, but he remained in prison without bail for almost two years.

From 1990 Bhutto maintained pressure on the government of Sharif by calling for new elections. By July 1993 there were fears that serious violence would break out. The army reportedly assured Bhutto and her supporters that both President Ishaq Khan and Prime Minister Sharif would resign, which they did later that month. A general election was held in October and was closely contested by Bhutto and Sharif. Neither won a clear majority, but Bhutto was elected to head a coalition government. Following charges of corruption and economic mismanagement, however, her government was again dismissed after less than three years in office, and her husband was put behind bars with a host of cases filed against him.

Repeated allegations of corruption against her have made little dent in her popularity. She lives in self-exile in the United Arab Emirates, refusing to face corruption charges filed against her in Pakistan's courts.

When elected prime minister of Pakistan in 1988, Benazir Bhutto became the first woman ever elected premier of a modern Islamic state.

The United Nations has been administering a ceasefire line in the disputed state of Jammu and Kashmir since 1948. Pakistan and India both claim the right to all of the state.

THE PROBLEM OF KASHMIR

When India and Pakistan gained independence, it seemed likely that the princely state of Kashmir would end up in the new Pakistan. Rulers of princely states could choose whether to join Hindu India or Muslim Pakistan. The Hindu ruler of the region, which has a Muslim majority, remained undecided before eventually signing Kashmir away to India. Pakistan refused to accept Kashmir's annexation to India and invaded, only to be met by the Indian army. Kashmir ended up divided with approximately two-thirds in India and one-third in Pakistan.

Jammu and Kashmir, as the state is officially known, remains a bone of contention between India and Pakistan. India accuses Pakistan of encouraging and arming the Muslim Kashmiri freedom fighters seeking secession from India. India's reluctance to negotiate with Pakistan on the future of Kashmir is largely motivated by a fear of the likely consequences. India also faces demands for secession from various groups in other parts of the country, and any concession to the Kashmiri separatists would be encouragement for others.

The situation reached crisis level when Mikhail Gorbachev, then the president of the Soviet Union, ended the war in Afghanistan in 1989. Weapons that once would have gone from Pakistan to the Afghan rebels went instead to Kashmir, and the result was a dramatic and tragic escalation of violence.

GOVERNMENT—PASHTUN STYLE

Among the hill Pashtuns, who live in the isolated mountains astride the border with Afghanistan, there is a style of informal government that has remained unchanged for centuries. In some respects it is anarchic, as there are no written laws and the rule of the Pashtun government extends only as far as main roads and a few villages and forts. The central Pakistani government is represented by a civil servant known as the political agent (PA), who exercises many of the functions of a governor.

The PA does not, however, interfere with the workings of the *jirga* (jerh-GAH), the Pashtun equivalent of a local council or parliament. The *jirga* is made up of indigenous group leaders, and while its decisions are final and irrevocable, there is a strong democratic element in that no one person can control its decision-making processes. Decisions are made on a consensus basis rather than a simple count of hands. Such a procedure reflects the underlying dynamics of the *jirga*, which is to arrive at a decision that will satisfy and be accepted by all the parties in conflict. Sometimes the *jirga* will meet to decide a matter of communal interest, such as the location of a new mosque.

ECONOMY

WHEN PAKISTAN GAINED INDEPENDENCE, its economy was based mainly on agriculture. Although it still forms the largest sector in the country's economy, agriculture makes up only a quarter of the Gross National Product (GNP) today. Karachi and Lahore have benefited from industrialization, while areas such as Baluchistan and North-West Frontier still struggle with subsistence farming.

Historical factors help to explain the slow growth of industry in Pakistan. In 1947, when Pakistan became a country, there were few factories, and the lack of an industrial base inhibited such development back then.

Left: Cotton is best picked by hand, which requires a lot of labor. In Pakistan, labor is cheap and plentiful. Workers like these Sindhi peasant women on their way home from the fields are employed to pick the cotton bolls off the shrubs.

Opposite: Men unload sacks of imported wheat at a port in Karachi.

Sheep play an important part in the Baluchis' struggle for survival. The fleece is made into clothes or woven into rugs and sold. The sheep also provide milk and meat.

BALUCHISTAN'S STRUGGLE

The western border regions of Pakistan are the poorest, and the level of economic activity has not changed much over the years. Economically, Baluchistan is the least-advanced region of Pakistan. The climate is very dry and does not easily support agriculture. Goats and sheep provide the main source of income, supplemented by a primitive form of agriculture that provides some of the basic necessities. Pastoral nomadism is still practiced in northwest Baluchistan, and camels and donkeys often provide the main form of transportation for the sparse population. Only a few green valleys in the south support crops, mainly of fruit, which is the chief cash crop and is exported to other parts of the country.

Nevertheless, Baluchistan possesses an economic potential that could one day benefit its population. There are substantial reserves of coal, sulfur, limestone, and other forms of mineral wealth in the region. Large reserves of natural gas were first discovered in the 1950s along Baluchistan's border with Punjab.

NORTH-WEST FRONTIER

Northwest Pakistan does not have the benefit of natural gas, coal, and other minerals and is heavily dependent on agriculture for its economic survival. Most people in this region are employed in agriculture. Wheat, sugarcane, and tobacco are the principal crops. The few industries that do exist are agricultural spin-offs, such as sugar-refining and food- and tobacco-processing.

When this region was under British control, it was considered to be of major strategic importance because of its proximity to Afghanistan and Russia. Consequently, road and rail networks were laid down to facilitate military communication and the transport of troops. This existing infrastructure has benefited the region's agriculture-related industries.

Two peasants carry harvested sheaves of wheat away from the fields in preparation for winnowing. The majority of Pakistani peasants have never heard of a combine harvester, and most farm labor is done without the aid of machinery.

PUNJAB AND SIND

The Indus River has not only provided rich alluvial soils, but has also facilitated extensive irrigation that now reaches what were once vast sandy tracts of desert. Today some three-quarters of Punjab's cultivated land is irrigated. Wheat, millet, rice, cotton, and sugarcane are some of the most profitable crops. Mangoes, guavas, and citrus fruits are the main fruit crops.

Sind's economy is also mainly agricultural, with basically the same kind of crops that are grown in Punjab. Sind has 205 miles (330 km) of coastline on the Arabian Sea, with backwaters that spread inland in all directions for hundreds of square miles. Both the coast and the backwaters are a rich source of fishing.

Unlike the western regions of Pakistan, both Punjab and Sind have important industrial areas. Punjab has highly industrialized areas producing machines and electrical appliances. It is also the region that produces many of the millions of bicycles, rickshaws, and automobiles used throughout the country.

Sugarcane is an important crop in both Punjab and Sind, regions blessed with fertile alluvial soil deposited by the Indus.

Sind's most important industrial activity concerns cotton and automobiles. The province produces one-third of the country's cotton output and two-thirds of its cars. Almost half of Pakistan's cotton textile mills are located in this region. The growing and harvesting of cotton, also found in the Punjab, plays a crucial role in the country's economy. Other industries in Sind include cement production and steelworks in Karachi. There are also many light industrial centers, some of which are built around workshops where artisans produce handicrafts.

PAKISTAN-UNITED STATES RELATIONS

The relationship between Pakistan and the United States has been largely influenced by Pakistan's nuclear policies and the United States' fight against first communism and then terrorism.

Nascent Pakistan faced Indian threats to its border integrity and national security and was embroiled in disputes with India over Kashmir. India was backed by the Soviet Union, which concerned the United States because of its communist ideologies. The United States and Pakistan became strategic allies during this period, known as the Cold War. The Cold War ended after the collapse of the Soviet Union in 1991.

In 1990 the United States imposed military and economic sanctions on Pakistan for possessing nuclear explosive devices. One of the effects of these sanctions was that the United States had to withhold $368 million worth of Pakistani military equipment, although the equipment had been ordered and paid for before 1990. A U.S. congressional amendment in 1995, however, eased the sanctions and led to the release of the equipment to Pakistan, among other allayments.

In 1998, India conducted nuclear tests, followed by Pakistan. This led the United States to place wide-ranging sanctions on both countries; even loans from international bodies, such as the International Monetary Fund (IMF), were cut off. After the September 11 attacks, the United States lifted its sanctions on Pakistan and India for their support in the fight against terrorism. Pakistan had interceded with the Taliban government in Afghanistan in a bid to capture Osama bin Laden.

MONEY FROM ABROAD

It has been estimated that Pakistan earns a large amount of foreign currency not through the export of some valuable commodity, but by means of its own people returning home with money earned abroad. Approximately 3.2 million Pakistanis work abroad as general workers as well as skilled technicians and professionals, and half of these are in the oil-rich Middle Eastern countries.

Large communities of Pakistanis live in the United States and the United Kingdom. Although permanently settled in these countries, they regularly send money to their families in Pakistan.

Pg 38: **Pakistani banks, like the Habib Bank in Karachi, are trying to juggle the demands of the modern financial world and the strictures of Islam.**

AN ISLAMIC ECONOMY?

After 1977, when General Zia imposed martial rule, a process of Islamization was begun that extended to economic aspects of life. An Advisory Council of Islamic Ideology was created with the responsibility of ensuring that the laws of the country were brought in line with the fundamental principles of the state religion. Among other matters, this involved making mandatory the *zakat* (zah-KAHT)—a tax on various types of personal income—and the *ushr* (OOSHR), a similar tax on land.

Muslim theology forbids the levying of interest on loans, and the Council was faced with the task of squaring this prohibition with a modern capitalist economic system. Proposals have been made to set up banks and other financial institutions that do not function using *riba* (ri-BAH), or interest, but there is also an unwillingness on the part of many of Pakistan's leaders to interfere too much with the conventional dynamics of the free-market economy. The government is considering the feasibility of setting up a parallel Islamic banking system to cater to the banking needs of the religious.

MILITARY ROLE IN THE ECONOMY

The Pakistan Army plays a significant role in the overall economy of the country. Directly and indirectly it is a stakeholder in many of the country's industries and in the real estate sector. The army owns high-tech ordnance factories, industrial machine-tool factories, aeronautical complexes and airlines; it has interests from banks to cereal factories and dairy farms, and joint-ventures with foreign investors in fertilizer manufacturing and oil refineries.

Generous allocations of prime agricultural land and urban real estate to army officers at highly subsidized rates have made military personnel key players in the real estate and housing sectors. Goods transportation is also a key economic sector for the army as it owns and operates trucks and services run by the National Logistic Cell, which has rapidly claimed a lion's share of goods transportation from the private sector as well as from the state-owned Pakistan Railways.

Some of the army-owned or co-owned enterprises include commercial and economic giants that are household names—Askari Commercial Bank, Shaheen Airlines, Fauji Fertilizer *(below)*, Fauji Cereals, and Askari Leasing—and prime urban real estate owned by district boards throughout the country.

ENVIRONMENT

FOR A COUNTRY TWICE THE SIZE of California, Pakistan boasts a diverse landscape, from craggy, snowcapped mountain ranges in the north to hot, arid desert plains in the Baluchistan plateau. The natural outcome of such diversity is a variety of habitats that harbors more than 3,000 animals and about 5,000 plant species. Half of these plants have great medicinal value.

ENDANGERED ANIMALS

Several of Pakistan's animal species are threatened or endangered. Some, such as the blind Indus River dolphin *(platanista minor)*, are unique to the country. This dolphin is only found in the Indus and is one of the most endangered dolphin species in the world. A combination of reduced water flow in the river, pollution, and increased human activity have gravely affected the population of the Indus River dolphin. There are estimated to be only a few hundred left.

Other animals, such as the snow leopard, blackbuck, and a variety of pheasants, including the shy Western tragopan, are either protected or listed as vulnerable. The snow leopard is hunted for its bones, which are said to be of medicinal value, and its fur. As a predator, the snow leopard is also killed because it is a danger to livestock.

In most cases the survival of an animal species is directly linked to the conservation of its natural habitat. In its effort to conserve species and their habitats, the government has established 225 protected areas, which together cover about 10 percent of Pakistan's total land area. Despite the government's efforts at conservation, many animals and natural habitats remain threatened.

Above: **A herd of blackbucks. The females and the young are usually light in color, while males are brown and become almost black with maturity and have spiral horns.**

Opposite: **A snowy mountain in northern Pakistan provides a scenic backdrop to an apricot orchard. Apart from plantations and orchards, trees are not common in the country.**

The houbara bustard's range extends from northern Africa to China. Its population is declining due to human activities such as hunting.

HOUBARA HUNTING   Success stories about conservation of the environment are few and far between in Pakistan, where the average citizen is more concerned with their own survival. The story of the houbara bustard *(Chlamydotis undulata)*, while not strictly a success, is an encouraging step in the right direction.

The houbara bustard is a bird that migrates to Pakistan every winter from its breeding grounds in Central Asia in search of warmer climates. It arrives in Pakistan every October and leaves in March and can usually be found in Baluchistan, Sind, and Punjab provinces. The houbara bustard measures up to 26 inches (65 cm) long and can weigh up to 4 pounds (1.9 kg). The bird lives in harsh and arid climates with little vegetation and can easily camouflage itself in its rocky and earth-toned surroundings. This ability unfortunately challenges houbara bustard hunters rather than discourages them. Every year hunting parties from the Middle East arrive in Pakistan to hunt the bird. In their own countries, the houbara has been hunted to near extinction. The bird is prized for its tasty meat, which is believed to be an aphrodisiac. The hunting parties use trained falcons and modern equipment to catch the houbara bustard. The lavish hunts flout Pakistani law, which lists both the houbara and the falcon as endangered animals. While Pakistanis are forbidden to hunt the houbara bustard, the ban is temporarily lifted during the migration season every year for certain foreigners, who are issued hunting permits. These foreigners are usually wealthy Arabs who can afford to reward the Pakistani government generously for the hunting permits. The government claims that this money can be used to benefit the welfare of Pakistanis.

Apart from being hunted, the houbara bustard is captured and exported to Middle Eastern countries for use in falcon training. Many birds can die during the journey. In addition, the houbara bustard's habitat is decreasing as deserts are developed for agriculture and other projects.

In a move to counter the destructive effects of houbara bustard hunts, conservationist Syed Babar Ali led World Wildlife Foundation (WWF) Pakistan against Arab falconers in the early 1990s. Their media campaign managed to bring conservationists from the United Arab Emirates to Pakistan in 1994 to discuss the houbara bustard issue. The following year the Houbara Foundation International Pakistan was set up to eliminate hunting of the bird and help it breed. The foundation later founded two research and rehabilitation centers in Punjab and Baluchistan to help with this work.

Nevertheless, the bird's existence remains in jeopardy. An unstable political environment and frequently changing priorities by successive governments have kept such nongovernment organizations from working effectively with the government toward formulating a long-term protection strategy for the houbara bustard.

Falconry is an age-old tradition in the United Arab Emirates. Once, skilled falconers let their falcons loose on smaller birds of prey to help augment their food supply in the harsh desert. The Arabs now regard the hunt as a sport.

MANGROVE FORESTS

Mangroves are salt-tolerant plants that grow in estuaries along the coastline. The Sind coastline has about 97 percent of Pakistan's mangrove forests. These forests provide a unique ecosystem for such organisms as birds, fish, reptiles, amphibians, crustaceans, and mammals, and protect the coastline from wind and tidal action.

Mangroves are used as fuel by those who live on the coast, but this activity now poses a threat to the mangroves. In addition the country's mangrove forests and marine environment were adversely affected by a crude oil spill in July 2003.

A Pakistani worker carries a basket of oil-contaminated sand during a clean-up operation at Clifton Beach. Greek ship *Tasman Spirit* ran aground off the Karachi coast on July 28, 2003 after moving into a shallow channel. It carried 67,535 tons of crude oil, 28,000 tons of which spilled into the sea. The ship broke in half two weeks later.

DEFORESTATION

Rapid deforestation has been taking place across the country. Pakistan has a variety of forests, but World Conservation Union Pakistan estimates that less than 5 percent of the country now remains under forest cover. Even this is decreasing at an alarming rate of 3 percent a year. At this rate, the country's forests are in danger of disappearing within the next 15 years. Years of unchecked logging, which provides fuel for a majority of rural households, has contributed to the problem, but the real threat to Pakistan's forests are people who exploit loopholes in the legislation to fell trees for commercial profit.

The threat to Pakistan's biodiversity is a result of pressures from a high population growth rate, an economic system that does not value the environment, a low literacy rate (46 percent), and a basic lack of ecological awareness. In a poor country where the average man is focused on his daily struggle for survival, conservation of the environment, to many, is a totally alien concept.

A large number of households in Pakistan use wood as a fuel for cooking and heating. This contributes to deforestation in the country.

Pakistan has six times the particulate matter suspended in its air than the World Health Organization (WHO) standard. The country does not have a proper system to monitor pollution levels in its air and water.

AIR POLLUTION

Pakistani cities have extremely high rates of air pollution. The main sources of air pollution are vehicular emissions, industrial production processes, and the unchecked burning of fuel and garbage.

Many vehicles in Pakistan run on diesel, which can be very polluting if the engine is not tuned properly. Smaller vehicles such as motorcycles and rickshaws also contribute to the problem; their two-stroke engines produce a lot of emissions.

To prevent air pollution by vehicles, compressed natural gas (CNG), which is found in great quantities in Pakistan, has been introduced as an alternative to petroleum-based fuels. Compared to other fuels, natural gas produces little soot and lower levels of carbon dioxide when burned. Pakistanis are slowly converting to this new, alternative fuel.

In 2001 about 170,000 vehicles were fitted for CNG use out of the 1,000,000 vehicles on the road. CNG filling stations are being constructed in Pakistani cities in phases.

GARBAGE OR GOLD?

Pakistan's largest metropolis, Karachi, produces more than 6,000 tons of solid waste daily. Managing such huge quantities of waste is no easy task. However, an informal system of recycling has evolved, and it seems to be working. Every day, almost 800 tons of waste is sold to junk collectors who pick up dry waste from people's homes. Another 700 tons is picked up by scavengers who go through waste in dumps, street corners, drains, alleys, and markets. The waste collected consists mainly of paper, glass, rags, bones, plastic, and metal. These are sent to recycling factories and are later made into items such as bottles, boxes, and machine parts.

This informal recycling industry plays an invaluable role in garbage

collection and disposal. It also plays an important part in Karachi's economy by providing employment to about 50,000 families. The informal recyling industry is estimated to produce over a million tons of recyclable material per year.

A local woman, Nargis Latif, took the concept further. A former journalist, she saw that the waste disposal problem in Karachi was getting out of hand and started Gul Bahao, a nongovernmental organization. It set up the Safai Kamai (Earn by Cleaning) Bank where people can sell their dry waste for cash. The Safai Kamai Bank is not a conventional bank but is instead a place where garbage can be deposited and exchanged for money and stored for recycling. People who bring a certain amount of garbage are given small gold coins.

Gul Bahao also works with wet garbage, but on a limited scale. Waste that consists of vegetable peels and other food is used to produce compost, which is sold to farmers. Despite receiving a warm response from citizens, Gul Bahao's expansion is limited by a lack of resources.

Young Afghan refugees in Pakistan form the bulk of the scavengers who sift through garbage and salvage 700 tons of recyclable waste daily.

PAKISTANIS

THERE ARE FIVE MAJOR GROUPS of people in Pakistan; three of them are named after the regions they predominantly inhabit. However, such a neat summary cannot do justice to the complexity of the ethnolinguistic groups in Pakistan. Successive waves of invasion and the assimilation of those who stayed behind have brought an astonishing array of people into the country. Persians, Greeks, Central Asians, and Arabs have, over the centuries, complicated the racial mixture of the country's population. Differences between the major groups are sometimes dramatic and can be seen in physical features as well as dress and language. Despite this, there is a unifying sense of being Pakistani, which comes in part from a common religion that helps define a shared set of values.

Opposite: **A cobbler sits in a local market with a fellow Muslim Pakistani.**

Below: **Schoolboys from the northern Chitral Valley sit with their textbooks under the shade of a tree. Public schools are segregated—boys are taught by male teachers and girls by female teachers.**

THE PUNJABIS

With approximately 73 million people living in the land of the five rivers, Punjabis make up 58 percent of the country's population. This numerical superiority, along with their occupation of the most fertile and prosperous region of Pakistan, explains why Punjabis constitute a large proportion of the country's political and social elite. Punjabis also figure prominently among the leading military figures who play an important role in the government of the country. This dominance is resented by minority groups. President Zia ul-Haq and Prime Minister Nawaz Sharif were Punjabis.

A young girl of Punjabi heritage.

More than half of Punjab's 1.2 million farms are owned by small farmers. The situation is different in Sind province, where aristocratic landowning families still dominate, and peasants have to give a percentage of their harvest to their landlords as payment for cultivating the land.

Punjabi men in the cities wear the *salwar kamiz* (sahl-WAHR kah-MEEZ), a suit that consists of a long tunic and a pair of wide trousers. On the head, a turban is normally worn, except in informal situations. Female Punjabi dress is not distinctively different from that of Pakistani women generally, namely the *salwar kamiz* worn with a *dupatta* (doo-PAHT-tah), a scarf.

THE MUHAJIRS

Muhajir (moo-HAH-jir) refers to the Muslims who came to Pakistan at the time of Partition from India. In 1947 Muhajir families packed up their belongings and either took a train or walked across the border to Pakistan, braving violence along the way. Many left India because they owned small businesses and felt that their livelihoods would be threatened in a predominantly Hindu state. Being commercial-minded and relatively better educated, the majority of them settled in Karachi, which was then the capital, and reestablished their enterprises in the form of family businesses. Many Muhajirs also settled in the other large Pakistani cities: Lahore, Multan, Quetta, Rawalpindi, and Hyderabad. They now form 8 percent of Pakistan's population. To some extent they still see themselves, and are sometimes viewed by other Pakistanis, as outsiders.

Two factors emphasize their difference from the majority of Pakistanis. Although the Muhajirs came from different parts of India, a unifying factor among them was Urdu, Pakistan's national language, which is spoken by a majority of Muhajirs. Most Pakistanis, however, have to learn Urdu in school. Another factor that has helped cause anti-Muhajir resentment goes back to the days of Partition. As the Muhajirs were arriving in Karachi, thousands of Hindus were leaving, fleeing across the new border to India. Although a minority in the city, Hindus held commercially important positions; these positions tended to be filled by the enterprising Muhajirs. The Muhajirs were also the most active in seeking the Partition and held important positions in the newly-formed Pakistani government. Resented, they were jostled out of the government by the Punjabi majority. Muhajir control of the Karachi city council ended in 1992. Sindhis rose to dominance, their strengh boosted by Benazir Bhutto who came to power in 1993 and based her party in Sind.

Muhajirs suffered greatly during the upheaval of Partition and as a result have grouped themselves into a community that wields enormous social and political influence. Pervez Musharraf, Pakistan's president since 1999, is a Muhajir.

Above: **A Sindhi woman takes a break from work to sit and meditate.**

Opposite: **A young Sindhi man wearing the traditional embroidered cap and *ajrak*. The *ajrak* is like the Scottish tartan—each tribe or clan has its own distinctive pattern and the male members wear their colors with pride.**

THE SINDHIS

The economy of Sind is based on agriculture. Parts of the province receive the bounty of water and fertile soil from the Indus River. Other parts, however, have to rely on canals and other means of irrigation. These have fallen into disrepair. World Bank grants in 2002 put in motion efforts to improve the agricultural infrastructure in the province.

Apart from agriculture, the Sindhis rely on livestock and fishing for a livelihood. Others work as laborers and odd-job workers.

In many of the small towns that have grown up along the rivers, there are families who trace their origins to countries such as Turkey and Afghanistan. Many place names include the word Shah, betraying their common Middle Eastern origin.

In some areas, wealthy landlords hold enormous social and political power, and peasants live a semi-feudal existence. It is not uncommon to find peasants suffering under a medieval type of servitude, being obliged

LIVING ON THE EDGE

In the peripheral areas of Sind, indigenous peoples live out their existence in ways that seem utterly remote from the early 21st century. In the western mountainous region, hereditary leaders, who command the loyalty of nomadic communities, make a home in places where a spring can be found. Their followers wander with their small herds of sheep and goats, while the women gather roots and berries along the way. The women also contribute to the small amounts of cash in circulation by weaving and embroidering carpets, rugs, and saddlebags that are then sold in market towns. Meanwhile, in the hot Thar Desert, there are the Koli, Meo, Vaghri, Mina, Bhil, and Hindu Rajput indigenous groups. Most of these people live in cone-shaped dwellings constructed out of the brushwood found in the desert. Here, too, blankets are woven by the women, while the men make pots and tiles. These groups of people make up a very small number of the Pakistani population, and their customs, dress, and lifestyle are far removed from that of most Pakistanis.

to give about 50 percent of their harvest to landlords. Modern agricultural innovations and irrigation projects worsen the peasants' plight. The new methods force many small farmers off the plots of land their families worked for generations. Landlords make more profit by cultivating larger areas of land, obtained by buying off numerous small landholders. In many ways the situation is similar to the oppressed plight of U.S. farmers described in John Steinbeck's 1939 novel *The Grapes of Wrath*.

The distinctive feature of male dress in Sind is the *ajrak* (aj-RUK), a colorful cloth about 6.5 feet (2 m) long and 24–36 inches (60–90 cm) wide, which is worn over the shoulder of the *kurta bizar* (KOOR-tah i-ZAHR), the long shirt and baggy pants worn by men. Individual groups weave their unique pattern into the *ajrak*, which is hand-dyed using vegetable dyes and cow dung. Another item of dress is the embroidered cloth cap with tiny mirrors stitched into it. Women, who do not wear the colorful caps, make up for it by embroidering their shirt-fronts with bright color schemes of their own. They also have a love for ornaments, especially gold.

THE PASHTUNS

The Pashtuns live in North-West Frontier and Baluchistan provinces. There are about 60 different groups, each of which is ruled by a chief and a council.

Pashtuns tend to be tall and strongly built with a high regard for fighting prowess. They have a justified reputation for being a warlike and rugged people. Disputes over property and personal injury often result in blood feuds between families. Within this social environment, the carrying of guns and knives is considered normal and expected behavior. In the 19th century, Pashtuns were the scourge of the British, who fought numerous battles against them in an attempt to secure control of the Khyber Pass. The British considered them the best guerrilla fighters in Asia and left them to be the buffer between British India and Russian and Afghanistan forces.

Some Pashtuns claim descent from one of the Lost Tribes of Israel, but many scholars believe they are the product of a mix of Aryans and other invaders.

The remote Pashtun ethnic groups are fiercely insular and conservative, and in some respects they live on the periphery of mainstream Pakistani life. Conflict with government agencies is common. For example, when plans were made for a new road to be built across land belonging to one group, resistance by the Pashtuns escalated into pitched battles with the authorities. However, this is becoming a thing of the past. Large numbers of Pashtuns now work in urban centers of Pakistan, Karachi being the preferred city. Former cricket star Imran Khan, now a politician, is a Pashtun; so are squash champions Jahangir and Jansher Khan.

THE KALASH OF THE HINDU KUSH

The Kalash people are a small group of about 3,000 who distinguish themselves from most other Pakistanis in a number of interesting ways. They live among the northern mountains of the Hindu Kush, and have their own language and dress, and practice animism, the worship of spirits in nature. Like many minority cultures around the world, their way of life is increasingly under threat as the outside world impinges more and more on what was a unique lifestyle. Over the years many Kalash have converted to Islam.

Festivals, weddings, and funerals are occasions for flamboyant displays of music and dance where the women, who are never kept in seclusion except during childbirth and menstruation, take to the dancing ground and perform traditional dances that have always excluded men. In their normal dress, Kalash women have a highly distinctive style characterized by the generous use of cowrie shells. The shells decorate a train that hangs from the back of the head to well below the shoulders. The embroidered train is covered with rows of the shells, interspersed with colored beads and coin-shaped pieces of metal, with the different shapes and sizes of the shells creating patterns that go across, up, and down the train.

In other respects, the role of Kalash women is highly circumscribed. Kalash villages have an area where women are forbidden to enter and partake in the religious ceremonies conducted there by the men. The beehive is seen as a paradigm of an all-male world, and consequently the eating of honey by women is forbidden. Women do have rights of their own, however. The idea of a broken marriage is acknowledged, and a woman can leave her husband, discuss the terms of a divorce, and remarry.

THE BALUCHIS

"If you spot a donkey, you've found a camp. If you only see a camel, then you are lost!"

—A Baluchi saying that reflects the importance of these animals to the nomadic Baluchis.

The Baluchis of Baluchistan are ethnically related to the Pashtuns, and it is difficult to observe any significant difference in their features. Similar to the Pashtuns, the Baluchis are fiercely independent and have proved just as resistant to change and bureaucratic control. They are semi-nomadic, and some clans have drifted into Sind and Punjab and taken up life as peasants. The Baluchis who retain a nomadic way of life are driven by the need to find fresh grass for their herds of sheep and goats and to avoid the punishing extremes of temperature. If lucky, a traditional Baluchi family will have its own horse. Donkeys and camels are kept for their usefulness in transporting goods.

The exact origin of the Baluchis is a matter of some dispute. The notion that, like the Pashtuns, they descend from one of the 10 Lost Tribes of Israel is as unlikely to be true as another theory that traces their roots back to Babylon. The latter theory is largely based on the similarity between the words Baloch, Baal, the Babylonian god, and Belos, one of the Babylonian rulers. It is more likely that Baluchis originate from the Caspian Sea region and traveled across Iran to reach present-day Baluchistan sometime in the 14th century A.D.

The Baluchis resemble the Pashtuns, but they are more likely to wear their hair and beards long. They have an aversion to egg-shaped skulls, and mothers will bandage and stroke their babies' heads in an attempt to mold a more rounded appearance. Distinctive features of Baluchi dress include a preference for white, suited to the arid and hot climate, and very large turbans, known as *pag* (PAHG), which use up to six feet (1.8 m) of cloth. Their baggy trousers, which require an even more generous length of cloth, use twice as much material as their turbans, and are worn under long robes.

The Baluchis have been adversely affected by economic developments that might have been expected to benefit them. Natural gas fields have been discovered in Baluchistan, along with coal, sulfur, and significant sources of various valuable minerals. The result has been a sudden surge of immigration from other regions of the country, and the native Baluchis have not gained much. Road-building and immigration have only served to disrupt their traditional way of life. A further bone of contention occurred when grazing lands in the east of Baluchistan were converted to cultivated fields fed by newly built irrigation canals. This too attracted new settlers, and in 1970 there was a violent uprising among some Baluchi tribes that led to the formal declaration of Baluchistan as the fourth province of Pakistan and the abolition of the princely states. The exercise was carried out through a military action, only to be followed by the Soviet invasion of Afghanistan, which resulted in thousands of new refugees.

Like the Pashtun *jirga* (see page 31), the Baluchi hold a council of leaders to discuss and decide on matters of importance to the community.

LIFESTYLE

FAMILY LIFE IN PAKISTAN is largely patriarchal and based around the extended family with three or even four generations living together. Wage-earning members of a family accept the obligation to care for those too old or too young to manage by themselves. There is generally a strong sense of family solidarity. Respect is always accorded to those older in years, and children are taught to obey their fathers and to go on obeying them even when they themselves are grown up and have children of their own.

While children are generally brought up in terms of obeying their elders, in other ways they are pampered. There are few family events to which young children are not invited, and their noisy presence at a party is always tolerated, even late at night. Young boys are particularly spoiled and receive preferential treatment. They are not expected to do as many chores as their sisters, and their misbehavior is tolerated where that of their sisters would earn a reprimand. Generally, children are introduced early to role patterns that will shape their adult behavior and attitudes.

Above: **In a typical city-dwelling Pakistani family, older women cover their hair with a** *dupatta* **or scarf while girls can wear their hair short and uncovered.**

Opposite: **A man weaves the colorful base of a wooden frame bed as children observe.**

The husband in a family is not likely to share in daily household duties. He will leave for work each day and return in the evening expecting his meal to be ready. This is accepted by everyone in the family and neighborhood as normal. When he has free time, he is most likely to spend it outside his home in the company of male friends. His wife is viewed as the family's daughter-in-law, and her household duties extend to taking care of her husband's family as a whole. In Pakistan's modern cities, however, the traditional pattern of family life is beginning to change. It is no longer a taboo for a young couple to live alone, and more would probably do so if financially secure enough.

THE STATUS OF WOMEN

Women are not seen as independent wage-earners, which explains the traditional preference for boys over girls. The birth of a son represents a continuation of the family line, a potential source of income, and an additional provision for old age. A baby girl, however, will eventually marry and leave. A woman who does not marry remains a constant burden on the family's income and sense of honor.

Women practice *purdah* (POOR-dah) in some parts of Pakistan, such as Baluchistan and North-West Frontier. A woman in *purdah* lives a life that involves almost complete segregation from the male world. She is never seen unveiled in the company of men except for her husband and close relatives. She never leaves her house unaccompanied, and always wears the *burqa* (boor-KAH), a full-length cover over the body and face.

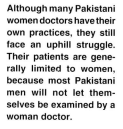

Although many Pakistani women doctors have their own practices, they still face an uphill struggle. Their patients are generally limited to women, because most Pakistani men will not let themselves be examined by a woman doctor.

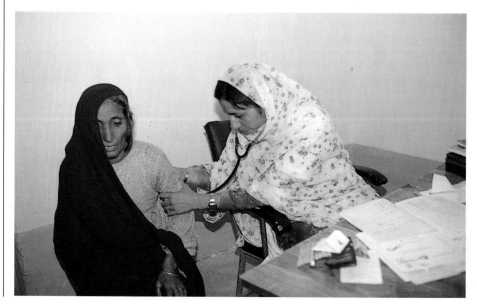

When it comes to skilled professions, women compete equally with men. Ayesha Rabia Naveed is Pakistan International Airlines' (PIA) first woman jet pilot.

The perceived status of women is deeply rooted in the Pakistani psyche. It reveals itself in the educational system, where only 25 percent of the female population attends school compared to 53 percent of males in the rural areas. This is very low considering that two-thirds of the population live in rural areas. Nationwide 53 percent of boys and 61 percent of girls never enter a school. An education is not considered necessary for girls by traditionally inclined families because employment that requires formal education is regarded as suitable only for males. There is also a feeling that "too much" education will only unsettle a girl by creating aspirations that cannot be fulfilled, as well as make her less attractive as a marriage partner among certain segments of the society.

The position of women in Pakistan is, however, very complex. A woman was elected prime minister in 1988 and 1993. Fatima Jinnah, the younger sister of Muhammad Ali Jinnah, ran for the presidency in 1965. Women have served as ministers in national and provincial governments, and women's movements campaigned for women's rights that were negatively affected by the Islamization that Zia-ul-Haq proposed. Also, Pakistan was one of the first countries to appoint women ambassadors.

THE BURQA

There are two types of *burqa*. One is made from black material and is a cloak-like, long-sleeved coat with a separate piece of cloth that covers the head and shoulders. The face is shrouded by three thin veils that are sewn onto the top of the black headscarf. Sometimes the veils are arranged so that only the top part of the face is visible, and sometimes two of the veils can be thrown back over the shoulder. This type of *burqa* is commonly worn by women from lower middle-class urban families and is considered quite fashionable.

The other type of *burqa* is more common in small towns and villages. It is white and also consists of two parts: a main shroud for the body made up of thick cotton, and a separate, tightly fitting headpiece. The face is covered by close-fitted netting that allows the wearer to see through it.

Women arriving at an office or factory remove the *burqa* and just wear the thin scarf known as the *dupatta* around their head and shoulders.

In rural areas where women work hard in the fields, the *burqa* is reserved for certain occasions, such as when they go out shopping. In the Punjab province, the picking of cotton is exclusively women's work, and wearing the *burqa* for this type of labor would be highly impractical.

The *burqa* is more of a lifestyle signifier than an item of national dress. Differences in style, especially regarding how much of the face is visible, have more to do with social class and a woman's view of herself than anything else. In urban, middle-class areas, the *burqa* is regarded as old-fashioned, and some emancipated women have their hair cut short and wear no *dupatta* or scarf. People who are more traditional in their beliefs would regard the absence of any head garment as quite shocking. Benazir Bhutto, for instance, is never seen in public without some kind of scarf worn over her head, although many believe this is only a political statement.

CIRCUMCISION

Apart from his wedding day, this is the most important event in the life of a Pakistani male. But as it usually happens between the ages of 2 and 5, he is unlikely to recognize its significance at the time. Only among the poorer and more traditionally minded people is the event likely to take place at a later age. Most families arrange for the circumcision to take place in the hospital before the newborn leaves. In rural areas there is always someone, often the local barber, who is experienced at performing the procedure (without anesthesia), and he is called on when necessary.

The act of circumcision is a religious requirement for male Muslims, and the event is celebrated by a feast. Better-educated, urban families are likely to arrange a party at home for members of the family and close friends. In the countryside, by tradition, the whole family as well as neighbors and friends attend the feast that takes place after the circumcision. The child will be dressed in his best set of clothes and will receive small gifts of money from the guests.

A rural man, dressed in his best clothes and the traditional decoration, on the way to his wedding.

MARRIAGE

Marriage is less a social and emotional bonding between two individuals and more a tie between two families and a source of prestige for everyone involved. Arranged marriages are taken for granted, and the bride and groom may often be surprised at the choice made for them by their parents. In some parts of the country, a marriage is arranged even before the couple is born, nor is it unheard of for a couple to see each other for the first time only on the day of the wedding. In urban areas, however, this is now regarded as old-fashioned and undesirable. Instead, once an engagement has been formally announced, the couple may start to go out together, usually accompanied by a chaperone such as the girl's sister. The agreement of the couple is looked for before any formal arrangement is made. Many parents will not go ahead with the match if there are strong objections by either party. Young people are brought up, though, to think of love as something that develops within a marriage, not as a precondition for it. In rural areas a woman marries before she is 20; in cities, a few years later.

The dowry is an essential part of a wedding. Traditionally, it consisted of gifts of jewelry and clothes, but today items such as refrigerators and television sets are just as likely to be featured. The higher the family is on the social scale, the more valuable and prestigious the dowry becomes, but for all parents it is financially the most demanding time of their lives. Usually it is up to the bride's parents to provide the dowry, but in some ethnic groups the groom's parents present the dowry to the bride's family. The cost of the wedding party itself, often involving hundreds of guests, is mostly borne by the bride's parents.

Before the wedding, the bride remains inside her house, while her family and friends prepare for the big event. Before the actual wedding day the most important event is the *mehndi* (meh-HEN-dee) ceremony. *Mehndi* is henna, a plant that produces a dye used to color the hands and feet. The henna is symbolically applied to the hands of the bride by the women in the groom's family. Afterward the henna is washed off and then reapplied by someone who is able to expertly create elaborate floral designs on the hands and feet. The importance of the *mehndi* ceremony derives from the formal coming together of the two families and mostly unfolds in two stages. First, the bride will stay at home while her family visits the groom's house, and then, the next day, the groom remains indoors while his family visits the bride's house where the *mehndi* ceremony takes place.

The wedding party is always hosted by the bride's family, and the beautiful decoration of the food is a matter of pride.

The wedding itself is a sumptuous affair characterized by a lavish party, often held a few days after the civil formalities in which official papers are signed. The newlyweds remain formally seated throughout the festivities and eat separately from the main body of guests. At some point in the evening, the couple will ceremonially depart for the groom's house, traditionally in a palanquin (a covered couch), but nowadays it is just as likely to be in a decorated car.

DEATH

Relatives and friends arrive at the home of the deceased as soon as possible after receiving the news. They wait outside the house until close relatives have paid their last respects and then enter to offer condolences by the side of the departed one, after which the body is wrapped in a white shroud, sprinkled with rose petals, and taken to be buried.

Women do not accompany the body to the burial ground. Men carry the body on a stretcher, or in the case of a young child, the father carries the body in his arms. At the cemetery the final prayers for the repose of the deceased are said. Muslims are not buried in coffins; the body is placed in the grave and the face is covered before it is lowered into the ground. A plank is placed between the body and the earth. Male relatives sprinkle the grave with earth before raising a mound above it.

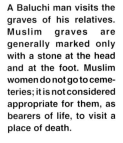

A Baluchi man visits the graves of his relatives. Muslim graves are generally marked only with a stone at the head and at the foot. Muslim women do not go to cemeteries; it is not considered appropriate for them, as bearers of life, to visit a place of death.

HOSPITALITY

The family is at the heart of Pakistani life. Public life in Pakistan is in many ways impersonal and cold, but this is partly because citizens reserve their warmth and sociability for the confines of their own homes. This does not breed selfishness and insularity, however, for the concept of the guest plays an important role in the family. Any family that can afford the expense will have a special guest room where visitors are invited to spend time with the family. Such a special room is a rather grand manifestation of the need to acknowledge the importance of showing hospitality to a guest. The same respect for a visitor is found among the poorest of families.

The giving of small gifts to a guest is a common observance among Pakistani families of all regions and classes. It may only be a piece of cloth, but it represents the tremendous respect that is accorded any visitor to a Pakistani home.

Among the indigenous Pashtuns, showing hospitality to visitors is one of the cornerstones of their social code. In a house built of mud and stone, even a group leader himself will stir the milk in a visitor's tea and add the sugar as a mark of his humility in welcoming someone into his home. Each Pashtun village will usually have a house with dormitory beds built for the sole purpose of accommodating guests.

"I despise the man who does not guide his life by honor." These words of the Pathan poet Khushal Khan Khattak may sound old-fashioned, but they are still revered by the Pashtun people.

Opposite: **An American journalist once asked an armed Pashtun whether it was really necessary to carry a loaded pistol. "Why do you Americans have nuclear weapons?" the Pashtun asked in response. "Is it not to keep peace in the world? I carry a gun so no one will bother me." It is a rare sight to see a Pashtun without a gun or rifle.**

THE PASHTUN CODE OF HONOR

Honor is central to the Pakistani value system, and among the Pashtuns it is practiced with a zeal and commitment that sets them apart. Their code for living is called *Pukhtunwali* (PUK-tuhn-wah-lee), and the notion of acting honorably is its basic tenet. This involves avenging any insult against self, family, or tribe. Although not inscribed in any statute, it has the same force as a law and is expressed in the proverb: "He is not a Pashtun who does not give a blow for a pinch." Sometimes an honor dispute will continue from one generation to the next. Whole families have been wiped out in this manner. The need for the aggrieved party to achieve satisfaction and justice takes primacy over the need to punish the aggressor.

Another feature of the Pashtun lifestyle is the concept of *melmastia* (mel-MAHS-tyah), which obliges all Pashtuns to provide hospitality and protection to their guests. Pashtuns greet their guests with pleasant expressions and usually treat them to dishes of meat, rice, and dessert. In addition, the guest is afforded protection by the host for as long as he stays within the the host's territorial responsibility. Similar to the concept of sanctuary, *melmastia* insists that anyone asking for protection should receive it unconditionally. This means that a criminal, arriving in a Pashtun village, can claim sanctuary from the police. It also means that enemies of the Pashtuns can arrive at their homes and demand protection; Pashtuns regarded the colonial British as enemies, but when some British people sought refuge at Pashtuns' homes, they were not turned away. An entire village can take up arms to protect a stranger who has claimed sanctuary.

The concept of honor is so important that Pashtuns use it, instead of racial origins or a common language, as a definition of their own identity. One is considered a Pashtun if one adheres to *Pukhtunwali;* one who shows a wanton disregard for the honor code is not a Pashtun.

THE RICH AND THE POOR

The lowest social class consists of people who earn their living as cleaners. The work of a paid cleaner, whether for a private house or the public streets, is generally considered beneath the dignity of a Pakistani Muslim. It is usually Christian converts and Hindus who do this work, which makes them social outcasts shunned by society at large.

The cleaners are careful not to touch things while they handle dung and human refuse. Sometimes they go about their work with their faces covered by a shroud because of the stench and filth they handle with their bare hands. Being a cleaner is something to be ashamed of. No one would willingly marry a cleaner except another cleaner, and as a group they tend to live in the poorest part of any town. Their wages are the lowest possible; this is reflected in the ghettos where they live. The only time they receive

Cleaners generally live in the slums of the city.

A middle-class Pakistani family sits together in a Persian-carpeted room to play carom, a popular board game.

some acknowledgment is at Christmas, when the Christians among them sing carols outside the houses they clean and receive a small amount of cash as a bonus.

At the other end of the social spectrum are the millionaires and near-millionaires. Their wealth often derives from the vast tracts of farming lands they own or the lucrative jobs they hold in urban centers. The Bhutto family is one example of this class. During the 1960s, 22 aristocratic families controlled nearly all of Pakistan's wealth. New wealth has since been created by successful business owners in the major cities.

The lifestyle of the very rich has little in common with the rest of the population. They live in big houses on exclusive estates and drive luxury cars. Children of such families go to private English schools, often completing their education in private boarding schools or prestigious universities abroad. Their acquisition of Western values and ways of thinking extends to styles of dress, another factor that separates them from ordinary citizens.

RELIGION

RELIGION PLAYS A LARGE PART in the life of most citizens. The country was established as an Islamic state in 1947. Millions of Muslims left their homes in India and made their way to the new country. There are a few non-Muslim minorities, and they have the right to religious freedom.

ISLAM

The prophet Muhammad began preaching Islam in Mecca around A.D. 610. He was, however, met largely with hostility. He eventually had to leave Mecca because its inhabitants were plotting to kill him. The flight of Muhammad from Mecca to Medina is called the *Hijra* (HIJ-rah), and the Muslim calendar is dated from that year, 622. Unlike the Meccans, the people of Medina received Muhammad warmly and embraced his religion.

Opposite: **A Muslim man ponders over lines in the Koran in the silent solace of a hall in a mosque.**

Left: **The entrance to the Badshahi Masjid, the second-largest mosque in Pakistan, built in 1674 by the Mughal emperor Aurangzeb.**

At the prescribed times, devout Muslims will stop to say their prayers, no matter if they are at a friend's house or in the middle of the Thar Desert.

RETURN TO MECCA Eight years later, Muhammad and his followers returned to Mecca and occupied the city in the name of Islam. Since then, Mecca and Medina have been the sacred cities of Islam, and most devout Muslims hope one day to be able to visit Mecca.

Islam spread outward from Mecca to the east and west. In 711 a Muslim Arab general conquered Sind. He brought with him the message of Islam that had been memorized and written down into a holy book, the Koran. Muslims believe that the Koran is the word of Allah Himself, revealed to Muhammad by an angel. Allah means God in Arabic. The Koran spells out the primary and absolute unity of Allah, who sends out prophets with sacred books designed to educate people about their duties to Allah and to each other. Muhammad is considered the last prophet, having been preceded by Adam, Noah, Abraham, and Jesus, among others.

Islam and Christianity share many beliefs and customs. Both stress the importance of compassion for the poor, and in Islam the giving of alms to the poor is one of the five Pillars of Faith. Muslims are obliged to give

THE FIVE PILLARS OF FAITH

- Belief in the oneness of Allah and the prophethood of Muhammad
- Five daily prayers
- The giving of alms to the needy
- Fasting during the month of Ramadan
- Pilgrimage to Mecca for able-bodied Muslims who can afford it

a percentage of their income to those in need, and in Pakistan this is deducted by law from bank accounts unless otherwise desired by the account holder. Both Muslims and Christians believe that life on earth is a preparation for the afterlife and that one's behavior on earth will determine the course of life after death. According to Islam, the record of a person's life will be presented on Judgment Day. If the record book is placed in the person's right hand, which indicates that a good life was lived, then a place in heaven is secured. If placed in the left hand, the person is condemned to punishment in hell.

Many children are sent to the mosque after school for religious lessons.

In Islam the graphic or three-dimensional representation of human or animal figures is prohibited. Other rules include the prohibition of gambling, eating pork, and drinking alcohol. Charging interest for the lending of money is also forbidden. This is a problem for a modern Islamic state like Pakistan. In December 1991 the Federal Shariat Court, set up to review the country's laws in the light of Islam's teachings, confirmed that charging interest was illegal. The court recommended that all financial laws be amended to conform with this, and 20 different laws were affected.

The ruling of the Federal Shariat Court is just one example of the work of the Council of Islamic Ideology. The council has the difficult task of arriving at interpretations of Islamic law that will be acceptable to many Islamic sects in Pakistan. Since there was no organization to set down a unified set of laws before 1947, slightly varying interpretations have evolved among the different sects.

ISLAMIC CUSTOMS

Devout Muslims everywhere pray five times daily facing the *Ka'bah* (KAH-bah) in Mecca. The *Ka'bah* is a small cube-shaped building inside the Great Mosque. It is sacred because it was here that Muhammad stripped the site of its former pagan idols and established it as the spiritual center for Islam in the tradition of Abraham.

The exact times for prayer—before sunrise, afternoon, late afternoon, sunset, and night—are symbolically announced from the minaret, the tower of a mosque. Nowadays this is likely to be an electronic recording relayed through loudspeakers, but by tradition the announcer is a crier known as the *muezzin* (moo-EZ-zin). The announcement, called the *Azan* (ah-ZAHN), takes the form of the declaration of the first Pillar of Faith: "I bear witness that there is no God but Allah and Muhammad is His messenger," and calls the faithful to come to pray.

Friday is the special prayer day throughout the Muslim world, and most male Pakistanis try to visit a mosque for afternoon prayers on that day. Before praying on a clean mat, there is a ceremonial washing of the face, hands, and feet. The prayer leader, the imam, faces the *Ka'bah* in Mecca and the worshippers stand behind him. Most mosques are not open for prayers to women, but if they are, the women will stand in a segregated section and join in the recitation of passages from the Koran. Ritualistic movements take the form of bowing from the hips and kneeling with the face to the ground. Most women conduct their prayers in the privacy of

The *muezzin* announces the *Azan*, calling the faithful to prayer.

their homes, also on a mat and facing the *Ka'bah* in Mecca. Any visitor to Pakistan, as in most other Muslim countries, will discover a small arrow positioned on the ceiling of the hotel room indicating the direction of Mecca as an aid for prayers conducted in the room.

Most Muslims hope one day to be able to make a pilgrimage to Mecca. Such a visit, called *Haj* (HAHJ), is commanded in the Koran, and every year Pakistani pilgrims fulfill this requirement by departing for Mecca in organized trips. The visit usually takes place over a short, two-week period during the 12th month of the Islamic calendar. In Mecca, the most important ceremony involves walking around the *Ka'bah* seven times and kissing the sacred black stone, a meteorite set into the east corner of its wall. After returning from pilgrimage in Mecca, a male pilgrim adopts the title *Haji* (HAH-ji) and may be addressed as such in public. Women earn the title *Hajiani* (HAH-ji-AH-ni), but it is rarely used as a form of address.

This elderly man is finally realizing a dream he has been planning and saving for most of his life—going on *Haj* to Mecca.

Colorful shrine offerings
on sale.

SHRINES

Shrines are frequently visited by Pakistanis searching for spiritual guidance as well as material help. Women who are threatened with divorce because they have not given birth to a boy, for instance, will repeatedly visit a shrine and pray devotedly in the hope that their wish will be fulfilled. Padlocks will sometimes be fastened to the grille of a shrine and opened only after the devotee's wish has been granted. Shrines are built around the tombs of saintly individuals and are often elaborately decorated by grateful worshipers. The tomb itself will be festooned with flowers, and the surrounding shrine building will be decorated with small mirrors and other embellishments. Hundreds of people will gather at shrines, usually on a Thursday evening, to listen to the chanting of religious songs. All the saints have their own festivals—called *urs* (OORS)—when thousands of devotees converge on a particular shrine to celebrate the anniversary of the saint's death. Special buses bring in worshipers from distant localities, and others trek for miles across deserts to be present at such an occasion.

One of the most important shrines is the mausoleum of Syed Usman, Shah of Marwand, known as Lal Shahbaz Kalandar. Usman arrived in Pakistan in 1260 from his native Iran, and when he died in 1274 his tomb quickly became a shrine, being added to and embellished over the centuries. Today, the mausoleum is a large building covered with blue glazed tiles and silver spires on the domes. Outside the shrine Muslim fakirs take up the yogic position and calmly meditate as hundreds of other devotees pass by on their way to visit the shrine. Annually, on the anniversary of Usman's death, the shrine is the focus for a festival attended by people from all over the country.

The shrine of Rukh-e-Alam in Multan.

Another important shrine is Bhit Shah, or the Mound of the King, 31 miles (50 km) north of Hyderabad. It was built in memory of a rich man by the name of Shah Abdul Latif who was a great poet and mystic.

Setting up of shrines, tomb visits, devotion to saints, and fakirs are some characteristics of Sufism, a movement within Islam that has elements of mysticism. Certain Sufi activities and beliefs are considered to be heretical by scholars and orthodox clerics. Sufis, however, have made important contributions to literature, calligraphy, architecture, and music. *Qawwali* (keh-WAH-lee), the mystic devotional songs of Sufi poets, are sung to this day in countries such as Pakistan and have a popular following. Similarly, there are stories, poems, and prose that were penned by Sufi poets and writers from centuries past that are still quoted now.

A Shiite man reading the Koran in a mosque. Shiites are a minority in the Islamic world.

ISLAMIC SECTS

Most Islamic sects fall under the two major groupings of Sunnis and Shiites. These two groups originated in a seventh century split over who had the right to the caliphate. Ali was the fourth caliph to succeed Prophet Muhammad after he died in 632. Ali was also the Prophet's son-in-law. Disagreements occurred throughout Ali's rule—one in particular resulted from his willingness to settle a conflict peacefully. This caused some of his followers to turn against him and form their own group. Ali was assasinated by a member of this group in 661. Following Ali's death, some Muslims were of the opinion that the next caliph should be Ali's (and therefore Prophet Muhammad's) descendant. Later known as Shiites, they believe Ali and his descendants have a divine right to be the true leaders of the faith. The majority, however, felt that the caliphate should be awarded to a person who was capable of being a good leader and imam.

Shiites constitute a minority in the Muslim ranks both in Pakistan and the world at large. The majority of Muslims are Sunnis, who believe that Ali was only one of the caliphs destined to lead the religion in accordance with the *Sunna* (SOON-nah)— the example of the Prophet. Sunnis and Shiites share many religious beliefs, although Shiites have their own clerics and tend to worship in their own mosques whenever possible. Shiites commemorate *Ashura* (AH-shoo-rah), the anniversary of the martyring of Muhammad's grandson Hussein, in a more dramatic manner than Sunnis.

THE PESH IMAM AND THE CLERIC

An imam is the chief officer, or attendant, of a mosque, and a cleric is a scholar of Islamic law. Together they make up the nearest arrangement in Islam that compares to an organized priesthood. Unlike priests, pesh imams are not required to undergo any formal religious education or training. An imam is generally selected from among the religious and respected men of the district surrounding the mosque.

The pesh imam's main duty is to lead the prayers at a mosque, but he also has a role as an informal adviser on religious and personal matters. People will seek out the local imam if they have a religious matter they wish to discuss. On special occasions, the role of the imam at public prayers may be taken over by a distinguished visitor, someone noted for religious piety or scholarship.

Clerics, who are the learned interpreters of Islamic law, are known by more than one name. As a general group they are known as the *Ulema* (OO-lay-mah), while those who tend not to share their traditional attitudes sometimes refer to them as *mullah* (MOO-lah). A cleric is revered not so much for his level of education as for his conservatism and his claim to know best how to interpret God's law.

There is no simple distinction between law and religion in Pakistan, and consequently the clerics often perform a political role. In some rural parts of the country their influence can be tremendous, and most local politicians would not wish to offend them unnecessarily.

RAMADAN

Ramadan (rah-mah-DAHN), also known as *Ramzaan* (rahm-ZAHN) in Pakistan, is the ninth month of the Muslim calendar and is the holy month of fasting. For 30 days, Muslims may not eat or drink from dawn to sunset. The only exceptions are nursing mothers and the sick, and they are expected to make up the lost days when able.

The season of the year in which Ramadan is observed changes every year because the Islamic year is 11 days shorter than the Gregorian calendar year. Fasting is a very demanding requirement that calls for considerable self-discipline, yet the majority of Pakistanis endure it with goodwill. It is very much a communal act of devotion. Each evening, once the *Azan* from the mosque has been sounded, food stands everywhere are busy with customers, as the fast may now be broken. In the early hours of the morning, the women of the house are out of bed preparing a hot meal to be consumed before the sun rises.

MOSQUES

The word mosque comes from the Arabic word *masjid* (MAHS-jid), meaning a place of prostration, pointing to its primary function as a place for prayer. On Fridays, mosques throughout Pakistan are crowded with men coming to pray, but individuals stop in on other days of the week for private prayer or a quiet conversation with friends in the courtyard. Compared to many churches, interiors of mosques appear functional; a *mihrab* (MIH-rahb), which is a niche pointing toward Mecca in front of which the prayer leader stands, and a pulpit for the imam are the main features. The main aesthetic attraction is provided by the colorful artwork that may decorate the walls. Outside the main entrance, and usually in a courtyard, a fountain is provided for the ceremonial washing that is required before prayers.

A distinction can be made between the bigger types of mosques, known as Jamia mosques, and the numerous neighborhood ones that can be found close to a community or town. The Jamia Masjid in Karachi is one of the largest in the country, with a capacity of 10,000. Even this, however, is small compared to the Faisal Masjid in Islamabad. It is reputed to be the largest mosque in the world, holding over 15,000 people under a vast, tent-like sweeping roof and many thousands more in its sprawling courtyards.

Mosques have also developed social and educational functions. Groups of children are taken there after school for religious instruction, something like traditional Sunday school in a church. In areas where there is no elementary school building, the mosque may serve that purpose. In the evening, groups of women may gather for their own religious instruction.

The unrivalled Faisal Masjid in Islamabad has minarets 290.4 feet (88.5 m) high that have been compared to rockets because of their modernistic design. The mosque, which also houses an Islamic university, was named after King Faisal of Saudi Arabia. The Kingdom of Saudi Arabia provided most of the $50 million that went into the building of the mosque, designed by a Turkish architect.

RELIGIOUS MINORITIES

Non-Muslims make up 3 percent of the population, and these consist mainly of Christians and Hindus. Relations between the majority Muslims and the minority religious groups were harmonious until General Zia started the Islamization process. In 1985 blasphemy laws were put in place to protect Islam from being defiled or defamed. However, these laws have been abused to incriminate people from religious minority groups.

The U.S.-led war in Afghanistan in 2001 sparked hate crimes against Christians in Pakistan. The shooting of 18 people who were attending a worship service in a Punjab church on October 28, 2001, was said to be the worst against Christians in the country.

Relations between Hindus and Muslims in Pakistan are affected by the relations of their counterparts in India. Hindu attacks on Muslims and mosques in India prompts violence against Hindus and their temples in Pakistan. Disputes between the two countries' governments over Kashmir have also contributed to tense communal relations.

Pakistani Christians at a church service.

President Musharraf has taken steps to rein in militant organizations that have been responsible for acts of violence against religious minorities. However, these have proved to be insufficient in ending such acts.

LANGUAGE

OVER 300 DIALECTS AND LANGUAGES are spoken across Pakistan, and not one of them is spoken by the entire population. Not surprisingly, the variety of tongues is the main factor dividing the various cultural groups. As the groups are regional in nature, so too are their languages. Sind is an exception to this. In recent years the region has received a substantial number of immigrants from other parts of the country. They go to Sind because of the better employment opportunities in both the cities and the countryside, and the native Sindhi language is spoken along with Punjabi and Urdu, making it easier for newcomers to adjust.

English was established as the language of bureaucracy and law in the 1956 Constitution, and its official status was confirmed in the 1962 Constitution. The 1973 Constitution, however, set 1978 as the year in which Urdu would replace English as the official language. Since then the use of English has decreased considerably.

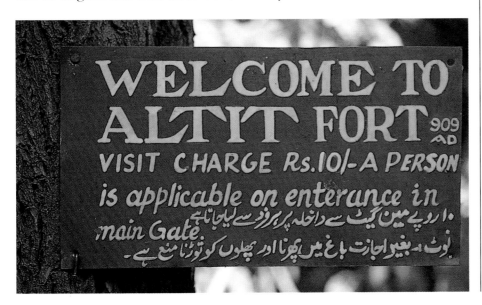

Opposite: **A street in Lahore is crowded with colorful advertisements and signs.**

Left: **A sign announcing admission charges for a tourist spot. Since Urdu was made the official language of Pakistan there has been a decline in the use of English.**

Rural Hunza schoolboys learning their numbers.

URDU

Urdu is the country's official language, but it is not indigenous to Pakistan and is used as a first language by less than 10 percent of the population. This is despite the fact that it is the medium of instruction in schools.

Urdu was the language of the educated Muslims of northern India, many of whom played large roles, especially economically and politically, in the creation of Pakistan. Due to its nationalist connotations, it has been promoted as the unifying language.

Urdu is an old language with a literature of its own. Literary Urdu reveals Persian and Arabic influences, and this is the chief difference between

Urdu and the Hindi language, which is written in a script descended from Sanskrit. Urdu, which is descended from Hindi, took on many of its characteristic features soon after the arrival of Muslims in northern India in the 11th century. A large number of Arabic, Persian, and Turkish words entered Hindi through interaction with Muslim military camps and commercial dealings with traders.

Over time, this hybrid language evolved into a separate dialect written in the Arabic script, with new letters added for sounds not represented in the original script. Eventually this dialect became known as Urdu, meaning camp language in ancient Turkish, and spread to become the common language of Muslims over much of India.

A man writes a letter for a woman whose husband is in jail for violating fishing rights. Only 31 percent of women in Pakistan are literate.

PUNJABI

Punjabi is an Indo-Aryan language. As the name implies, it is spoken in the Punjab region, a historic territory that is now divided between Pakistan and India.

Many different dialects of Punjabi are in use, numbering at least several dozen. The major ones are Western Punjabi, mainly spoken in Pakistan, and Eastern Punjabi, spoken in India. One Punjabi dialect spoken in Pakistan, known as Lahnda, is considered sufficiently different from the mainstream language to warrant classification as a separate language.

Originally, the written Punjabi language, in the then secret Gurmukhi script, was used to record the teachings of the 10 Sikh gurus, the founders of the Sikh religion. The Gurmukhi alphabet (which means coming from the mouth of the guru), was invented in the 16th century by one of these gurus. Gurmukhi is still used by Sikh Punjabi speakers in India. Muslim Punjabi classical writers always used the Urdu script to pen their literary works. Punjabi, however, is not often seen in its written form in Pakistan and occurs more commonly instead as a spoken language.

SINDHI

This language is spoken by about 16 million people in the southern Pakistani province of Sind. Hyderabad, one of Pakistan's largest cities, has the greatest concentration of Sindhi speakers in the country. Across the border in India, there are an estimated 3 million speakers of the same language. Sindhi is related to Urdu, and in Pakistan it is written in a special variant of the Arabic script, with additional letters to accommodate special sounds. Two factors have contributed to the diminishing numbers of Sindhi speakers, one being the number of non-Sindhi speakers who have settled in the province. Most urban areas now have a majority of Urdu speakers. The other factor goes back to the days of Partition in 1947, when many of the educated Sindhi speakers, who were Hindus, left the province for a new life in India.

Left: **A teacher and his students in a classroom in Sind.**

Opposite: **Although Punjabi is widely spoken and understood by a majority of Pakistanis, children like this young Punjabi girl learn to read and write in Urdu when they go to school.**

When the Soviet Union invaded Afghanistan in 1979, as many as three million Afghan refugees crossed the border into northern Pakistan. Many from the first few waves found work as peasants, but the majority of them stagnated in refugee camps like this one.

PASHTO

Pashto is the language of the Pashtuns, and while it has been spoken by them for centuries, there was no written script of the language until recently. An attempt has been made to remedy this and help preserve the rich oral tradition of the language. Thus a modified Persian script has been introduced. The large numbers of Pashto-speaking Afghan refugees, who fled Afghanistan when it was invaded in late 1979 by the Soviet Union, have helped spread the use of Pashto in Pakistan.

If you think you have had enough of the sweet tea or pastries that have been offered to you, just say "bus" (BOOS), which means enough.

ACH'HAA?

Despite the hundreds of languages and dialects spoken across Pakistan, there are certain words and phrases that are used and understood almost everywhere. *Roti* (ROH-ti) means bread, and it is understood as such almost everywhere. This flat bread, in all its versions, forms such a basic food in Pakistan that the word is sometimes used to represent the broader concept of eating or a meal. So, for example, a traveler or guest may be invited to join a group of men eating by being greeted with the words *roti khaao* (KHA-o), which literally means eat bread.

Even more ubiquitous is the use of the term *ach'haa* (ahch-CHAH) which means good. It has a far wider meaning, though, and includes the friendly and amicable spirit that Americans express when saying okay or no problem. What really stretches its meaning, however, is the way one or both syllables can be drawn out to indicate varying shades of expression. A few examples follow:

Ach'haa?	Really?
Ach'hha	That's all.
Aach'ha!	Nothing more to say; that's okay; understood; okay.
Ach'hhaah!	I'm shocked!

ARTS

PRE-MUGHAL STYLES can be seen at ancient sites, such as Mohenjo Daro and Harappa, and in Taxila where the Buddhist Gandhara art is believed by many to bear Greco-Roman influences. The arrival of Islam further enriched Pakistani art, especially architecture. In other areas of the arts, Islamic theologians have mostly discouraged artists from engaging in pictorial art because realistic paintings and statues might be seen as divine in their own right and divert attention from the worship of Allah. Also, Allah is regarded as the only creator of life, so any attempt to create realistic forms is seen as blasphemy. But this prohibition has not always been followed, and Pakistani art represents both Islamic and modern Western influences.

Above: **A Pakistani putting the finishing touches on the tilework adorning the exterior of a mosque.**

Opposite: **A close-up of embroidered patchwork. Pieces of patchwork like this may be used to make bags, cushion covers, quilts, or wall hangings.**

DESIGN MOTIFS

Traditional Islamic art has been compared to modern forms of abstract art. Despite their divergent origins, the two approaches have in common an emphasis on abstract patterns and geometric shapes. The most distinctive Islamic art form is the arabesque, an ornamental style in which linear flowers, fruit, and designs are represented in intricate patterns. The arabesque was introduced to the region around 1000 B.C. from the Middle East and is greatly in evidence in modern Pakistan.

The focus on geometric patterns and designs has produced what is probably the world's most complex and sophisticated development of this art form. People outside Pakistan are only able to appreciate it by way of lavishly illustrated books and visits to art museums. In Pakistan itself, the art is on public display in the colored tiles and the incredibly elaborate designs that weave their way around the exterior and interior of mosques.

CALLIGRAPHY

The language of the Koran is Arabic, and this flowing script was used by the early Muslims when they first recorded the words. This beautiful writing has been developed into an art form and has inspired a calligraphic art. Short extracts from the Koran are written on large scrolls and hung in the interior of mosques. The lavish flourishes of calligraphy are a beautiful sight. Sometimes the calligraphy is surrounded by elaborate designs or arabesques to complement the words.

There are two main styles of Arabic calligraphy: Kufi and Neskhi. The Kufi style is the older form. It developed in Iraq and flourished until around the 12th century when the Neskhi style became more prevalent. Both calligraphic scripts are used to make copies of the Koran, with the older style being reserved for the chapter headings. In Pakistan, Arabic, Persian, and Urdu can also be found on nonreligious objects such as vases and plates. This is particularly true for most non-Arab calligraphy, which is centered around classical poetry.

POTTERY

Pottery is the oldest art form in Pakistan, going back to the time of the Indus Valley civilization, as excavations at Mohenjo Daro have revealed. Many of the techniques in use today were perfected more than 1,000 years ago in Syria and Iraq and brought to Pakistan by Muslim artists. Chief among these techniques is the engraving or painting of intricate lattice designs on the clay slip—an undercoating on the object—and then overglazing it with

Many mosques are adorned with ornate calligraphy, either with the name of Allah, one or more of Allah's 99 attributes, or with a verse from the Koran.

transparent glazes of different colors. Another technique, introduced into Pakistan from the Middle East and still practiced today, involves the application of blue designs on white ceramic glazes—a demanding technique that Italian potters copied during the Renaissance.

The art of the potter is also in evidence in the beautiful tilework adorning the minarets and domes of mosques as well as the walls of public buildings. Tile-making is traditionally a family occupation, with the skills handed down from generation to generation. Around Hyderabad, such families still practice the techniques first acquired by their ancestors centuries ago.

An astonishing continuity in artistic traditions can be found in the work of contemporary potters applying their skills and imagination to the production of kitchen plates, vases, and other decorative items. Motifs and animal designs that were discovered in Mohenjo Daro, and which date back nearly 5,000 years—including lattice designs, floral patterns, leopards, bulls, and rhinoceroses—still appear.

In Pakistan, pottery skills were traditionally handed down from father to son, but today there are many women potters.

95

Pakistan's carpet exports brought in only $160 million during the first nine months of the 2003–04 fiscal year compared to $233 million during 2001–02. This decline is partly due to the return of Afghan refugees in Pakistan to their homeland after the fall of the Taliban government in 2001. Afghan refugees are cheaper than local labor. Before they returned to Afghanistan, they made up half of the workforce in the carpet industry.

CARPET-MAKING

Carpet-making in Pakistan and India flourished under Mughal rule in the 16th and 17th centuries. Mughal emperor Humayun introduced Persian art by importing rugs from the country. His successor, Akbar, set up carpet workshops in Pakistan and India and brought in carpet weavers from Persia to tap on their knowledge and experience. Jahangir and Shah Jahan also supported the carpet-making industry in their time.

The close link between art and everyday life in Pakistan is dramatically apparent in the work of carpet-makers. Although carpet factories exist, many people work in their own homes and take the finished product to a carpet company where it is checked for quality and then paid for. Whole families often work together to make carpets.

Rugs and carpets are made mostly for daily use. In indigenous areas they are woven from camel hair and wool mixed with cotton. This type is known as the *farshi* (FAHR-shee) rug. The patterns are never drawn down. The women who do the weaving discuss the choice of colors and patterns among themselves before starting work. The designs and patterns that carpet-makers employ vary from region to region. In regions that border on Afghanistan, the Kalashnikov rifle was used as a motif on carpets during the war that followed the Soviet Union's invasion of Afghanistan. Certain basic designs and motifs are ubiquitous—wavy lines with abstract patterns, geometric shapes enclosed in squares, and octagons—but the scope for variation and invention seems endless and identical carpets never seem to appear, other than from the same factory or family.

Pakistani carpets are finely knotted and of high quality. Very expensive carpets may take as long as a year to complete and may cost tens of thousands of dollars. Lahore, Karachi, Multan, and Hyderabad are the major carpet-manufacturing centers in Pakistan.

CHILD LABOR IN THE CARPET-MAKING INDUSTRY

Children are especially valued in carpet-making because their small hands and agile fingers are supposedly ideal for tying the fine knots used to create the patterns. Unfortunately, unscrupulous merchants exploit children for this type of work. The children are forced to work long days on looms and are paid very little, if at all. Many are driven by poverty, and sometimes parents sell off their children for this kind of work in an attempt to pay off outstanding debts. Child labor is prohibited by law but violations still continue. However, the carpet-making industry is receiving assistance from foreign and international bodies to eradicate or reduce the use of child labor.

The Shish Mahal, with its mirrored roofs and interior walls, is one of the most eye-catching buildings in the Lahore Fort.

ARCHITECTURE

Classic Pakistani architectural design can be seen in the design of mosques and ancient buildings. Before the Mughals, there existed fine examples in architecture, mainly of Islamic tombs and shrines. A good number of tombs in southern Sind, such as Makli Hills near Thatta and Bhit Shah in Hyderabad, and Multan and Uch in Punjab, that were built from the 10th to 15th centuries are significant for their unique architecture. The tomb of Delhi sultan Qutubuddin Aibak, known for his famous Qutub Minar in Delhi, also belongs to the same period.

The Shah Jahan Masjid in Sind is impressively large, approximately 19,800 square feet (1,821 square m) in area, with over 90 domed compartments that help spread sound throughout the mosque. The acoustics are such that prayers recited in front of the *mihrab* travel around the whole building and can be heard in every corner. The entire interior is decorated with superb, painstaking craftwork—in the artwork of the pillars, the intricate patterns in the tiles, the glazed bricks of various hues and the beautiful calligraphy that adorns the gold-colored stonework everywhere. The carving of the stone is so fine and delicate in places that from a short distance it would seem to be the work of a sculptor working with soft wood.

The ancient city of Lahore is particularly rich with examples of the country's glorious architectural past. Mughal emperor Akbar made it his capital from 1584 to 1598 and started building the Lahore Fort, which was added to during the reigns of Jahangir and Shah Jahan. The Lahore Fort remains an eloquent testimonial to these illustrious rulers and also to a group of anonymous 16th century architects. The fort covers an area of 30 acres (12 hectares), and the buildings inside its walls serve to remind one of the rigorous class system that prevailed at the time. A special raised balcony was built in the *Diwan-e-Aam* (di-WAHN-e-ahm), the Hall of Public Audience, so that the powerful emperor could look down over his subjects who came to present petitions or beg for a favorable judgment in their disputes. Wealthier subjects, landlords, and rulers in their own right went to the *Diwan-e-Khas* (di-WAHN-e-khahs), or Hall of Special Audience.

The Shish Mahal—the Palace of Mirrors—is an extravagant outburst of the imagination. It was built as a home for Shah Jahan's wife Mumtaz Mahal and consists of a row of domed rooms with high roofs covered with hundreds of thousands of tiny mirrors. The mirror mosaics are in the style of the traditional Punjabi craft of *shishgari* (shish-GAH-ri), the designing of patterns from fragments of mirrors.

If not for the Taj Mahal in Agra, India, which Shah Jahan also designed, the Shah Jahan Masjid would be looked upon as his greatest architectural achievement. His reign, from 1627 to 1658, is synonymous with the finest expression of Mughal art.

METALWORK AND JEWELRY

Metalwork, like other arts and crafts in Pakistan, bridges the division between objects for everyday use and *objets d'art*. Platters and trays designed to be used in the home are often beautifully engraved with floral designs and intricate scrolls tapped out with light blows from a small hammer. Every large town has a shopping area where metalworkers sit cross-legged on cushions while they hammer out their designs on finely worked plates, teapots, vases, and other household utensils.

There is also a flourishing business producing decorative metalwork items, many of which are copies of famous medieval pieces of art. Different regions are famous for their expertise in highly specialized branches of metalwork. Certain towns in Punjab, for instance, are renowned for their damascene, metal ornaments inlaid with gold or silver. Another speciality is silver inlay on a metal amalgam, producing a startling contrast between the silver and the dark metal. Expert filigree work, using fine wire strands of gold, silver, or copper to form delicate tracery, appears on window frames, grills, and folding screens.

Jewelry is held in high regard and pieces are treasured and kept for generations. They are worn with pride by women, and often represent the entire wealth of a family. Poor families would never think of parting with valuable items of family jewelry. Chokers, earrings, bracelets, and necklaces are often made of solid silver, inlaid with emeralds and rubies.

A metal craftsman works painstakingly to engrave a tray with a verse from the Koran.

POPULAR ART

Popular art is on display, not in art galleries, but on the sides, backs, and fronts of the myriad vehicles found on the streets of Pakistan. The fascination with abstract forms and the creative play of colors, shapes, and motifs is readily apparent here. Realistic portraits of people, animals, plants, and places appear as well, as though the strictures of Islam that normally discourage such pictures did not apply in this context.

The paintings that sometimes adorn every available inch of space on a truck or bus are only realistic in the sense that the subject matter can be easily recognized, like a mountain landscape or a lush valley. Just as identifiable are the animals and fish that crowd in on one another like a crazily packed zoo.

Trucks and buses have become, literally, the art galleries of Pakistan.

This is where the photographic realism ends, however, for the colors and motifs that are also present go well beyond what is pictorially correct. Sunsets are not just red but flaming red, as if the earth were on fire. The colors used to paint animals are exotic, and the mixing of animals with floral patterns and stylized hearts, all enclosed within a waving border of lurid shapes, is surreal.

Religious symbolism is not absent. The word Allah in the Arabic script is a recurring presence, surrounded by floral displays or framed by an arabesque. Often verses from the Koran are painted on. A popular one is the prayer asking Allah to keep travelers safe.

QAWWALI

Qawwali *have gained popularity with Muslims who speak neither Urdu nor Punjabi, as well as with non-Muslims.*

Qawwali (keh-WAH-lee) are the mystic songs of Sufi poets, characterized by the rhythmic chanting of repeated phrases to the accompaniment of music. The singers of these devotional songs are called *qawwal*, and their aim is to strengthen the conviction of believers and convert nonbelievers to Islam. Traditionally, musical accompaniment is played on a *sarangi* (SAH-run-gi), but as this sometimes takes a half hour to retune between songs, modern performers prefer to use the harmonium instead. The harmonium is a cross between the organ and the piano accordion and is said to have been introduced to South Asia by Portuguese Jesuit missionaries who were seeking to spread Christianity.

A contemporary *qawwali* band consists of a lead singer, known as the *mohri* (MO-ri), two harmonium players, a backup singer, and a percussionist. The *qawwal* sing both ancient and modern *qawwali*, and a contemporary *qawwali* band will compose new songs and the music to accompany them. Sometimes, as in jazz, new compositions emerge during a performance. *Qawwali* are sung in Persian, Punjabi, or Urdu, and are usually staged on a Thursday evening, the eve of Islam's holy day, at a shrine or a Sufi meeting place. Women *qawwal* are nonexistent, although they are shown singing *qawwali* in movies.

The lyrics are usually devotional in nature, praising Allah, Muhammad, or Ali, Muhammad's son-in-law. Others praise the saints who introduced Sufism to the region. The poetry behind the devotion can be appreciated even in translation, with lines like "The dust of his footsteps is fragrant to my nose" and "Since you, my beloved, fell out with me, the birds no longer come to sing on the little wall."

Qawwal with a nondevotional, secular nature have emerged in recent years. Although criticized as shallow, these are easily marketable.

Nusrat Fateh Ali Khan believed qawwali *are for everyone.*

KING OF QAWWALI (1948–97)

Nusrat Fateh Ali Khan was Pakistan's premier *qawwal*. He was born in 1948 to a family with a long line of *qawwal*. His father, a famous classical musician who was also a *qawwal*, realized how demanding his own work was and wanted his son to study medicine. But the young Nusrat was captivated by the sound of his father's singing and started to take lessons. Nusrat came to be known as *Shahen-Shah*—meaning The Brightest Star—and received numerous awards, both in Pakistan and abroad. The Pakistani government honored him with the Pride of Pakistan award in 1986.

Nusrat Fateh Ali Khan performed in Pakistan and abroad, attracting a full house wherever he went and frequently attracting non-Muslims to his international concerts. He said, "It's great that even people who don't understand the language appreciate the music. It doesn't need words. I convey the message of the Sufi, the saints, but my music is not just for Muslims, but for anyone who believes in God. It's open to anyone."

Nusrat's band was made up of family members, and in Pakistan, it released a new audio tape every three months. For the international market, they brought out record collections titled *Shahen-Shah* and *Mustt Mustt*. He died in August 1997 in a London of heart attack. He had a history of liver and weight problems and had traveled there for medical treatment.

LEISURE

MOST FAMILIES IN PAKISTAN cannot afford to spend much money on leisure activities, and children are generally left on their own to develop enjoyable pastimes.

Kite flying is popular throughout the country. Kites are often homemade, and children learn through experience how to apply the aeronautical principles that make a successful kite. A discarded plastic bag and carefully selected twigs will be fashioned into a kite with the judicious use of glue, and it is a matter of pride to make one that stays aloft for more than just a short while.

Other games popular with young people include marbles and something that resembles hopscotch. In the cities there are more opportunities for entertainment, usually on the weekend. Coastal cities like Karachi have camel and horse rides on the beach, family picnics in the public gardens, and an amusement park with bumper cars and train rides.

Left: **A young boy realizes what fun it is to splash around in the canals that are part of the irrigation system in Punjab.**

Opposite: **A polo game in progress. Polo is played on horseback, and the aim of the game is to hit the ball into the goal using long wooden sticks.**

While every school has fields for cricket, field hockey, and soccer, the necessary facilities for tennis and squash are available only in private clubs. The club membership fees mean that only a tiny minority of Pakistanis have the opportunity to play.

SPORTS

Cricket is the national sport of Pakistan. Soccer and field hockey feature on the timetable of most schools, and although Pakistan's national soccer team has not achieved any notable success, the country's field hockey team is always a force to be reckoned with in international competitions. Volleyball, tennis, and squash are also popular games. Pakistan has had an extremely rich and successful tradition in squash, dominating the game through the 1980s and 1990s, while also producing great champions throughout earlier decades. Early star Hashim Khan quit school to play squash professionally at age 12. However, he first played in a major championship only at age 35 and went on to win the U.S. Open three times, the last in 1963 at age 48, well after other players his age were past their prime. He was the patriarch of a family of squash champions that includes Jahangir Khan. The latter won the British Open for 10 consecutive years from 1982 and played for five years without losing a game. In 1985 he even won two games in Britain and the United States in less than 24 hours.

POLO Polo is a stick-and-ball game played on horseback by teams of four players—although Pakistani teams tend to have at least six. The playing area, the largest for any ball game, is 300 yards (274 m) by 160 yards (146 m), although often the boundaries are not fixed and play extends over an even wider area. The object of the game is to strike the ball with a hand-held mallet into the opposing 8-yard-wide (7 m) and 10-foot-high (3 m) goal. Each game is divided into seven-minute periods known as chuckers, and the number of chuckers in a game varies from one competition to another.

Polo was first played in Central Asia around 500 B.C. When the game traveled east to the land south of the Himalayas, it took a firm hold, and when the British colonized the Indian subcontinent, they discovered the game and took to it with enthusiasm. It became a popular game with the British army, and most of the best polo teams today come from the armed forces of the United Kingdom. This is due in part to the fact that while only wealthy individuals can afford to own their own horses, the army and the police play as team members on horses that are not personally owned.

Polo is most popular in the northern areas of Pakistan, and large crowds turn up for the breathtaking displays of horsemanship that are a guaranteed feature of every game. The boundary is usually a low-lying wall, and the audience crowds dangerously close to this wall to follow the progress of the game as the ball is hurtled around the field and bounced off the wall at high speed. Pakistan also has the highest polo ground in the world at Shandur Pass.

Between 1960 and 1978, no cricket was played between Pakistan and India due to the dispute over Kashmir.

CRICKET Cricket was developed in England in the mid-16th century. It is a bat-and-ball game similar to baseball, with each team of 11 players taking turns to bat and bowl. The batting team's objective is to defend the wicket, made up of three wooden stumps placed at either end of a grassy 22 yard (20 m) pitch, against the bowler of the opposing team, who bowls a small heavy ball at the wicket. If the batsman hits the ball away, he can then run to the other end of the pitch and score a "run."

The British introduced the game to the region, and Pakistan now has one of the best cricket teams in the world. Pakistani cricket stars include Imran Khan, Saeed Anwar, and Zaheer Abbas.

It would be difficult to be in Pakistan between October and March without realizing that the cricket season was in progress. If Pakistan is playing at home in a test match, the host city often declares the final day of the match a school holiday. While the game itself may be played in Lahore, almost 500 miles (800 km) away, near the Afghan border, people will huddle around a radio listening with bated breath and roaring with delight at every run scored by their country's team.

While the commentary to an international match is blaring from every radio and television set in the country, boys will be lined up in teams, playing the game in a nearby field or side street. They hope to emulate their country's great cricket stars, who, unlike the majority of Pakistanis who achieve fame and fortune, were not born in the lap of luxury and privilege.

Sometimes the excitement and passion generated by a game of cricket goes beyond the matter of sport. Any encounter between the national teams of Pakistan and India can take on political overtones, especially if the political relationship between the two countries happens to be particularly tense at the time. In 1986, when Pakistan for the first time defeated India in a series played on Indian territory, the returning heroes were greeted by a crowd of over a quarter of a million.

CRICKET SUPERSTARS

Hanif Mohammad (1934–)

Hanif Mohammad has held two world records in cricket. Playing in a match between Karachi and Bahawalpur, he was running for his 500th run when the ball hit the wicket before he could reach it. The 499 runs represented the highest score ever reached in first-class cricket, and the record stood until it was bettered by Brian Lara of the West Indies, who scored 501 runs in 1994. In 1958, playing for his country against the West Indies, Hanif Mohammad conducted the longest innings—scoring 337 runs over a period of 16 hours and 10 minutes. By the time he retired in 1969, he had obtained centuries (100 runs in one inning at bat) playing against all the major cricket nations except South Africa (due to its apartheid policies). Hanif Mohammad was small for a cricketer and this earned him the nickname Little Master.

Imran Khan (1952–)

Imran Khan is considered to be one of the world's great all-rounders in the history of modern cricket. His fast bowling was feared by opposing batsmen, while he himself was well-known for his attacking style when batting. Imran Khan was 18 when he first played for his country against England. In 1987, when as captain of the national cricket team he resigned, there were demonstrations outside  his house calling for him to return to the game and captain the Pakistani team against the West Indies. Some fans even went on hunger strikes until he agreed to return. Eventually, after President Zia also called for his return, Khan agreed to come out of retirement. He then led his team to victory in the World Cup competition in 1992 before retiring from the game and taking up a career as a politician. He left the game as one of Pakistan's most successful captains.

According to the Guinness Book of Records, the greatest victory in cricket was when Pakistani Railways beat Dera Ismail Khan (another Pakistani team) by 851 runs at Lahore in 1964.

Boys on bicycles selling pictures of movie stars are a common sight in small cities and in the countryside.

MOVIES AND TELEVISION

If a family possesses a television set and a program is being broadcast, then the television will almost certainly be on. And it will stay on until the last broadcast is over. People do not necessarily watch what is on, and may go about their business—talking, sewing, cooking, eating, and so on—only occasionally pausing to watch something of interest. If visitors come into the house, the television will not be turned off or down, but simply ignored.

In the countryside television viewing has become the main leisure activity in the evening. In the past, farmers would go to bed soon after nightfall because there was little else to do, but now the television monopolizes their time until around 11 p.m. when primetime ends. Friends and neighbors who do not possess their own sets will drop in to watch their favorite programs.

Some television time is taken up with religious programs consisting of sermons or readings from the Koran. While readings from the Koran are treated with grave respect, the sermons by *mullahs* are open to jokes, especially if they are lengthy. More popular are the game shows, music programs, soap operas, and dramas that are churned out with relentless regularity from the movie and television studios in mainly Lahore and Karachi. Satellite television arrived in the

1990s, and soon thereafter came cable television. Indian channels were very popular on cable, especially in the cities. The government banned them in 2002, however, and several independent Pakistani channels started broadcasting soon after.

Movies are not made one at a time, as in the West, and a big star is often involved in a number of movies at the same time. The typical movie is a rich mixture of action, drama, suspense, romance, music, and dancing. It is a genre in its own right, with conventions that every Pakistani will understand and appreciate. An action sequence involving a high-speed car chase may be quickly followed by a scene in a rural setting with the hero being sung to by a group of dancing females. This may then be followed by the star singing a solo number in a very romantic mood, only to be followed by gunfire and a fistfight.

Crowds of people flock to the movie theaters on weekends. In the cities, going to the movies is a favorite form of entertainment. A new movie featuring one of the country's movie stars will attract huge crowds, and posters of the star will be seen everywhere.

STORYTELLING

Each cultural group has its own folk literature that has been passed down from one generation to the next by word of mouth. Stories about legendary or historical figures are still told by semiprofessional storytellers whose skill is not in telling a new story, but in retelling a familiar tale in a new style. Changes in the tone of voice, body language, and anecdotal extras all contribute to the audience's entertainment. Unfortunately, this tradition is now being eroded by the spread of television.

Punjab is especially rich in its store of romantic tales, and a recurring theme is that of doomed lovers thwarted by fate and parents who cannot understand the force of their children's feelings. The most enduring romance of them all is the story of Heer and Ranjha.

Men gather after work to listen to a storyteller. Stories are often composed in classical verse forms that lend themselves to singing.

HEER AND RANJHA

It was love at first sight when Ranjha first gazed into the eyes of the beautiful Heer. It happened that Ranjha was wandering aimlessly, having left his home after a family dispute. One day he came to a river and boarded a ferry, tired and exhausted after days of walking through unknown territory.

There was a bed on the boat belonging to Heer, and the boatman reluctantly agreed to let his passenger sleep there. When Heer boarded the boat, she was shocked to find a strange man in her bed. Her scolding awakened Ranjha, who opened his eyes to the sight of Heer and could only exclaim, "Oh, beloved!" She too fell in love instantly.

Each afternoon the lovers would meet by the river. Their love was kept a secret until a vindictive uncle told Heer's father what was happening. Ranjha was immediately expelled from the village, and the heartbroken Heer was forced to marry a man she did not love.

Ranjha sought help from holy men and a plan was worked out that involved Heer's sister-in-law, who also wanted to run away with her lover. The four young people all ran away the same night, but Heer and Ranjha were caught and put on trial. When it was revealed that Heer had been forced into marriage, her marriage was declared invalid and Ranjha and Heer were free to marry.

However, the wicked uncle was convinced that the familiy honor had been violated. As Heer prepared for her wedding day, he gave her a poisoned drink and she fell dead. Ranjha rushed to her tomb, and torn by grief and feeling there was no reason left to live, he fell dead on her grave.

FESTIVALS

THE MAJOR FESTIVALS in Pakistan are mostly religious, although there are many rural festivals that are more secular in nature. In the north of the country, the coming of spring is often celebrated with locally organized competitions. Pairs of oxen are yoked to the wheel of the village well and timed to see how long they take to complete a set number of turns. Music and fireworks add to the festivities. The day is welcomed by farming people who work hard throughout the year and have little leisure time. Later in the year, at harvest time, local festivals will be held again to mark the successful conclusion of another summer's work. In Punjab, this is the time when singers and storytellers bring traditional myths and legends to life. A popular folk dance is the Bhangra, which is usually featured at Punjabi harvest festivals. It is a dance performed in the open, and both men and women take part. Even if the harvest has been a poor one, and the crop yield is a disappointment, there will still be a festival. Pakistanis believe strongly in fate and do not place the blame on anyone for an event seen as part of God's plan.

Many festivals vary from one region to another. In a northern area called Hunza, the fall festival celebrates the return of the herdsmen from the higher pastures, and a sword dance is performed. The sword dance harks back to the lawless days of this once inaccessible region, when a man's survival depended on his ability to handle a sword in close combat.

The two major religious festivals are the two Eids. Choti Eid, or the Small Eid, celebrates the end of Ramadan, the fasting month, and 10 weeks later, Bari Eid, or Big Eid, commemorates Abraham's willingness to slaughter his own son in obedience to God.

Above: **During their spring festival, Kalash women take to the dancing ground and perform traditional dances that exclude men.**

Opposite: **Sindhi men clad in brightly-colored costumes perform a dance in a Karachi street.**

At Lahore's Badshahi Masjid on the eve of Eid, the courtyard of more than six acres (2.4 hectares) fills up long before sunrise and so do the surrounding gardens and streets. A crowd of 300,000 is not unusual.

EID AL-FITR

Young people always look forward to the Small Eid, the *Eid al-Fitr* (eed al-FIT-ER), because it is the time of the year when they receive a new set of clothes and gifts of money. It is more like Christmas in the West than any other Pakistani festival. Employees receive bonuses, factories and offices close for a couple of days, and food and money are distributed to the poor.

Eid al-Fitr, celebrated throughout the Muslim world, is the most festive day on the Islamic calendar. On the eve of Eid, thousands of Pakistanis set out on lengthy journeys to pray at one of the bigger mosques.

Small Eid is always an occasion for a celebratory meal because it marks the end of Ramadan, and family members start the day with a breakfast that might include a dessert of thin noodles cooked in milk with nuts.

On the first day of the festival, all the male members of a household visit a mosque for special morning prayers. Immediately after, they visit friends and relatives. Children, dressed in their best new clothes and looking forward to receiving gifts of money, also go visiting. During the festival the Pakistani love of dress is displayed to its best advantage by the various ethnic groups. Punjabi males wear new turbans, Pashtun men carry their best rifles, the barrels often painted, and even camels will be adorned with gaudy trappings. The women wear their best *shalwar kamiz* or traditional dress. Those who wear head-to-toe *burqas* dress in colorful new robes, while other women don new gowns of fine embroidered silk.

EID UL-AZHA

Eid ul-Azha (eed ool-a-ZAH), also known as the Big Eid, is the celebration of Abraham's willingness to sacrifice his son Ishmael in obedience to Allah. It is marked by the slaughtering of a male goat, sheep, calf, or a camel. Despite the cost, this is something no family will forego willingly.

The day itself begins like the Small Eid, with the men and boys going to the mosque for special prayers. When returning home they will bring with them a butcher to sacrifice the animal if they are not doing it themselves. Whoever carries out the slaughtering will preface the act with the words "in the name of Allah."

The sacrificial meat is cut into three main portions: for the family, for the relatives, and for the underprivileged. Charitable institutions receive large amounts of meat on this occasion. On the days that follow, the average family consumes more meat than at any other time of the year.

During both Eids, the usual greeting is *Eid mubarak* (eed moo-BAH-rak), meaning an auspicious Eid to you.

Fattened and decorated goats are on sale everywhere in the days preceding Eid ul-Azha.

On *Ashura*, devout Shiites participate in processions commemorating Imam Hussein's martyrdom.

MUHARRAM

On the 10th day of Muharram, the first month of the Muslim calendar, the death of Hussein, the grandson of the Prophet, is marked. Hussein was killed in 680 A.D. in the cause of Islam, during the religious dissension that inaugurated the split between the Sunnis and the Shiites. Within the Shiites there is further division between Twelver Shiites and the Ismailis. The Twelver group believes that the line of living imams came to an end with the 12th.

After the death of the sixth imam, Jaafar ibn Muhammad, the Shiites were divided as to whom should be the next imam. The majority accepted Musa al-Kazam, Jaafar's younger son, as the seventh imam. Some, however, were loyal to Ismail, Jaafar's eldest son. They splintered off to become the Ismailis.

The mourning begins on the first day of the month for Shiite Muslims, but the culmination of the festival is on the 10th day, known as *Ashura* (ah-SHOO-rah). On this day there are large public processions held in all parts of the country where Twelver Shiites are found. The most dramatic feature of the day is the self-flagellation that some extreme devotees suffer as an act of pious identification with the sufferings of Hussein. They cry "Ya Hussein," which means "Oh Hussein!" in grief.

Sunnis commemorate the death of Hussein in a less dramatic manner. For the first 10 days of the month all forms of public entertainment, including the playing of music, are shut down.

NATIONAL HOLIDAYS

March 23	Pakistan Day: The commemoration of the Pakistan Resolution passed in 1940 calling for a separate Muslim state.
May 1	Labor Day.
August 14	Independence Day: The commemoration of the founding of Pakistan in 1947.
November 9	Iqbal Day: The birthday of national poet Allama Iqbal.
December 25	The birthday of Muhammad Ali Jinnah.

The exact dates for the religious holidays, the two Eid and Ashura, are determined every year in conjunction with the lunar calendar.

MELAS

Melas (MEH-lahs) is the general word for the fairs that take place throughout the country at different times of the year. They are not national events and generally attract only the local population. To the visitor they often seem to represent a mix of the religious and the secular.

Traders set up more stalls in the market than usual, and a traveling circus may erect its tents to display dancing bears and monkeys. A merry-go-round is nearly always put up in the town or village square, to be followed by swings and slides. Women and children arrive at these *melas* in large groups.

In many areas, the arrival of *melas* mark the largest shopping days of the year, and many traders, like this carpet seller, set up stands to display their various wares.

There may also be an air of religious frenzy as people engage in chanting and ritual dancing. The biggest and most dramatic *melas* are those associated with Sufi saints. Every village in Pakistan has its own small shrine dedicated to a local saint, and every saint has his *urs*, the annual celebration dedicated to the memory of the holy man. Some of these festivals attract thousands of devotees from all over the country.

URS

The mausoleum of Syed Usman, known as Lal Shahbaz Kalandar, located in Sind, is the site of an annual three-day festival. What is unusual about Usman is that he is revered by both Muslims and Hindus. There are three guardians of Usman's shrine—one Muslim and two Hindus. The position of guardian-of-the-shrine is a hereditary one and remains in the same family for as long as there is a male to inherit the role.

Usman's death is commemorated by the enactment of a marriage ceremony representing the saint's communion with God. On the first day a marriage procession travels from the home of the Muslim guardian to the flower-laden tomb. Marriage processions are also carried out on the second and third days, starting from the homes of the Hindu guardians. Hindu and Muslim pilgrims come from all parts of Sindh and beyond, and for three days the air is full of music, dancing, and singing. In the courtyard of the mausoleum, large copper drums are beaten constantly as devotees make their way to the shrine. Both men and women dance, a traditional ritual set of movements that propel the dancer forward and backward with hands held high in the air. Usman is also the special saint to groups of singing women who have their own ritual display of song and dance that seeks to emulate the religious ecstasy of the moment of union with God.

BASANT FESTIVAL

Traditionally this colorful festival took place in Lahore and marked the coming of spring. Over the years Basant has become popular throughout Pakistan and is celebrated with great pomp in all the major cities.

Kite strings are sometimes coated with ground glass, and the object is to try and ground competitors' kites by cutting their strings in the air. Serious kite flyers wear finger patches to protect their hands. Every time a kite string is cut, a tremendous roar goes up from the appreciative crowd. Drums and trumpets are played to make sure everyone knows another competitor has been knocked out of the game. Basant lasts all day and into the night, and in the evening food stands are crowded with competitors and spectators. The following morning children can be seen climbing telephone poles and trees, trying to collect the fallen kites.

Glass-coated kite strings cause blackouts in cities when they cut electrical wires and can wound or kill people. The Lahore city council banned kite-flying for three months in 2003 to have time to draft legislation to control the popular activity and make it safer for everyone.

Kite-flying is a popular pastime but reaches a fervor during Basant. Rooftops, as well as big fields, become the locations for large-scale kite flying competitions. There are different competitions for different categories of kites, from small ones to those over three feet (1 m) long.

FOOD

THE FOOD OF PAKISTAN shares a common heritage with India, but there are a number of factors that distinguish the two cuisines and which help to identify the special nature of Pakistani food. First, Indian cuisine tends to focus on a vegetarian diet. Pakistani food is said to use more cooking fat and chili.

The Middle Eastern cuisines of Persia (modern Iran), Turkey, and the Arab states have left their influences on Pakistani food. The generous use of yogurt came from these countries to western Pakistan, providing a welcome cooling effect on the heat generated by the equally generous local use of chili peppers.

Lamb, chicken, vegetables, curries, rice, and bread are the mainstays in Pakistani meals. Fruit such as mangoes, plums, melons, apricots, peaches, and apples are common and sold by street vendors, while sweet desserts provide a pleasant close to meals.

Opposite: **A food vendor cooks his food in a street in Gilgit.**

MUGHAL CUISINE

The term Mughal food, with its aristocratic and exotic connotations, has become a general term for the style of cooking commonly found in Pakistan and northern India. To the average Westerner the food both sounds and tastes incredibly rich.

Chilies, turmeric, garlic, and ginger are relatively expensive ingredients in the West and used sparingly, whereas in Pakistan many of these are standard ingredients. Some of the more expensive items, such as saffron, are not readily available to ordinary people in Pakistan either, but the typically rich and hot curry taste can be produced by using chili peppers, garlic, onions, and tomatoes, which are abundant and inexpensive.

The basic curry consists of onions, garlic, and tomatoes cooked with small amounts of meat with spices and herbs in oil. What often lends a distinguished look to a curry is the garnish. Curries are garnished with a rich and varied selection of vegetables, spices, herbs. Raisins, cashew nuts, pistachios, and eggs usually accompany curries served at special occasions or feasts.

Bread is an important part
of the Pakistani diet.

BREAD AND RICE

About 98 percent of the daily diet of most Pakistanis consists of four basic items: *roti* (bread), rice, vegetables or lentils, and some meat.

Roti comes in a variety of forms, of which *naan* (NAHN) is quite common. Countless versions of the *naan*, a leavened flat bread, exist across a wide territory stretching from the southern regions of the former Soviet Union to north India. In Pakistan it is eaten for breakfast, lunch, and dinner, and can accompany nearly every dish. It is baked in a special oven called the *tandoor* (TAHN-door). A small coal or gas fire burns under the oven. The professional *naan*-maker shapes his bread to a thickness of about half an inch (1 cm) and then places it in the oven by hurling the bread against the hot sides of the oven, removing it later by means of a pair of iron tongs.

Paratha (pah-RAH-thah), a whole wheat griddle bread, is also popular. Along with regular whole wheat flour, *chapati* (chah-PAH-ti) flour, which is made from a wheat that is very low in gluten, can be used. The basic

THE NATIONAL DRINK

Most Pakistanis, being Muslims, do not drink alcohol. Tea, known as *chai* (CHAI), is the most common beverage and is drunk everywhere. It generally comes with the milk already added and is usually heavily sweetened. After a meal, jasmine tea is sometimes served.

Interestingly, despite being the most popular drink in Pakistan, the country does not cultivate tea. Pakistan spends $300 million a year to import tea from India, Sri Lanka, and Kenya, making it one of the world's largest tea importers.

Rural people drink a glass of milk if they can afford it, or lassi *(LAHS-see), which is yogurt mixed with water and crushed ice. Lassi is flavored with sugar for breakfast and with salt for lunch. Lassi is an ideal drink for summer as it has a cooling effect.*

paratha mix can be turned into a light puff pastry or a heavier, thicker version—both kinds can be served stuffed with minced meat or vegetables. Every home will have in its kitchen a rimless iron pan called a *tawa* (tah-WAAH) that is used for cooking the *paratha* or *chapati*. The skillful part of cooking these breads is in the kneading of the dough; the correct consistency must be reached before rolling out the dough into flat discs ready for cooking on both sides. Special breads include *shirmal* (SHEER-mahl), cooked with milk and eggs, and *roghni naan* (ROGH-nee), a soft and sweetish bread that accompanies many meat dishes as a delicacy.

Rice is the other staple in the Pakistani diet. Apart from plain white rice, one of the internationally known rice dishes is *biryani* (bir-YAH-nee) or *pulao* (POO-lah-o), a corruption of the original Turkish pilaf. This is cooked in a meat sauce and is a favorite dish across the country for special events and festive meals or for dining out. At its most attractive it is served with decorative pieces of edible silver paper that have a yellowish tinge due to the addition of a tiny amount of saffron. Even a plain-looking dish of white rice can taste delightful because of the judicious addition of cloves, cardamom, and cinnamon.

This fruit seller sits amid his wares, awaiting customers.

SHOPPING FOR FOOD

People in Pakistan buy their food in the local bazaar, a huddle of food stands and other small shops. Shops of the same kind are usually grouped together, so the meat-sellers will be in one group, fish vendors will occupy another area, and various displays of herbs and spices will also be found alongside each other.

An interesting feature of many meat and fish stands is the way the meat is cut up. The vendor squats on a small platform behind his cutting table, and customers find themselves at eye level with him. The meat or fish is purchased by weight and usually needs to be cut up in small pieces ready for cooking. A large, razor-sharp knife is held between the large and index toe of one foot. The vendor simply holds the meat in front of the knife and moves it around, its size determining how many cuts are required. More modern stands have a large, curved knife fixed in position on the table.

In every bazaar there are stands that sell only *roti* and curry. Practiced hands slap the dough around with the speed and expertise that comes only from experience. As the *chapati* or *naan* are baked, or the *paratha* is reaching perfection, the vendor will spoon an amount of lentil or bean curry into plastic bags where it will keep warm.

Fast food, with a considerable amount of the local variety, is also readily available on the streets of most towns from vendors who peddle their food from mobile carts. They are often found around schools or offices at lunchtime, ready for the onslaught of schoolchildren or office workers.

GLOSSARY OF INGREDIENTS

Saffron: This is obtained from the orange-red stigmas of an Asian crocus. It is very expensive, as 150,000 flowers are required to produce two pounds of saffron. Fortunately, only a pinch adds an intriguing taste to whatever is being cooked; when added to rice it produces a golden color. Saffron is not commonly available in Pakistan; it is an imported and expensive delicacy.

Cardamom: This is a tropical, perennial shrub, a member of the ginger family. Its aromatic seeds are highly flavored. It is a basic ingredient of most traditional Pakistani curries and is generally sold in its pod.

Turmeric: This is a rhizome of the ginger family. When fresh, it resembles fine, ginger-like fingers and is bright yellow on the inside. It is mostly available ground, as a yellow powder.

Coriander: This herb is used all across Asia, and while most countries just use the leaves, in Pakistan the stalks are also used to add flavor to curry stock. It is also known as cilantro or Chinese parsley. Coriander is used both in its green and powder form.

Cumin seeds: These are aromatic seeds used in small quantities to add zest to food.

KEEMA MATTER PILAU

3 cups long-grain rice
3 tablespoons oil or ghee
1 teaspoon cumin seeds
1 medium onion, finely chopped
1 clove garlic, crushed
$\frac{1}{2}$ teaspoon fresh ginger, finely grated
6 whole cloves
8 ounces ground beef
2 cups shelled green peas
4 cups hot water
3 tablespoons salt
1 teaspoon *garam masala* (gah-RAHM mah-SAH-lah), a powdered spice mix available at Asian groceries

Wash rice if necessary and leave to drain. Heat ghee or oil in a large, heavy saucepan with a tight-fitting lid. Fry cumin seeds, onion, garlic, ginger, and cloves in the oil until onion is soft and golden brown. Add meat and fry over moderately high heat until meat is browned. Add peas and half a cup of water. Stir well, cover and cook until peas are half done. Add rice and hot water and stir in salt. Bring to a boil, cover, turn heat very low and cook for about 10 minutes. Uncover and sprinkle with *garam masala*. Do not stir. Replace lid and continue cooking for another 10 minutes or until the liquid is all absorbed and the rice is cooked. Serves four.

PAKISTANI DISHES

BREAKFAST

Nihari (**NI-hah-ri**): This is a meat mixture made of beef, brain, tongue, and marrow blended together in gravy. It is often eaten with *naan*.

Halwa-puri (**HAHL-wah-poo-ri**): This is a light breakfast dish. Small balls of wheat dough are slapped and smacked into paper-thin discs and fried in oil, where they puff out like small footballs—this is the *puri*. The *puri* is eaten with *halwa*, a sweet made with semolina. They are made at home or bought from a food stand where they are served with lentils and gravy.

LUNCH OR DINNER

Korma (**KOR-mah**): Spiced meat served with yogurt sauce in a thick gravy; a favorite meal.

Machli ka salan (**MAK-li ka SAH-lan**): A fish curry.

Haleem (**HAH-lim**): A luxurious dish made of meat that has been cooked in seven grains including rice, different types of lentils, and wheat.

Tikka kebab (**ti-kah kuh-BAHB**): Cubed meat barbecued on skewers or baked in the *tandoor*.

Raita (**RAI-tah**): This yogurt sauce, seasoned with delicate combinations of chili peppers, coriander, and pepper, is the most common accompaniment to a hot curry and rice. Subtle variations in the taste are obtained by imaginative additions to the basic ingredients.

DESSERT

Mithai (**MI-thai**): This is the generic name given to a confection that comes in a variety of bright colors. Mithai includes *ladoo* (lad-DOO), *gulab jamun* (gu-LAHB JAA-man), *ras malai* (RASS ma-LAA-ee), and others. It is made from lentil flour, cooked in syrup, and may be garnished with nuts.

Barfi (**BAR-fee**): A fudge-like candy made from thickened milk flavored with coconut, almond, or pistachio and served in small squares. Candies like these are distributed to friends and neighbors on Eids and other happy occasions.

CHEWING PAN

Pan (PAHN) is a mixture of betel leaves, betel nut, and coconut attractively laid out on a green leaf that has been spread with a lime catechu paste. Betel leaves and nuts are imported from Bangladesh and Sri Lanka, despite increasing success in growing the plant in Sind.

Pan is not available in restaurants as it does not function as an accompaniment to a meal. Rather it is sold in stalls and shops that may also sell tobacco and soft drinks. A special counter facing the pavement is given over to the preparation of *pan*. More commonly, it is prepared and sold from a mobile street stand. People will often buy the *pan* to chew after a meal because it is said to aid the digestive process.

Pan sellers have to work hard to make a living out of selling an inexpensive condiment; a 16-hour day is not uncommon. The typical *pan* seller squats on a small platform surrounded by colorful bottles containing the various ingredients. Special mixtures using less common ingredients are available from some *pan* stalls, and for these more exotic *pans* a higher price is charged. While each vendor has his own style and recipes, the basic process is the same. Pan comes in many flavors, plain, sweet, and semi-sweet.

The *pan* vendor begins by taking in the palm of his hand one of his precut betel leaves and spreads a white lime and brownish red catechu paste on it. The various ingredients are added, and the final spread may be topped with a liquid syrup. The adept *pan* vendor then swiftly folds it into a compact little package. The customer places the little bundle in one side of the mouth and chews it slowly, allowing the various juices and flavors to work on the taste buds. *Pan* has been blamed as one of the agents that cause oral diseases, such as mouth cancer, in Pakistan.

The presence of tobacco makes pan *addictive, and it has become a daily habit for some people. The unmistakable marks of the habitual* pan *chewer are pale, yellowish-brown lips and teeth with a reddish-black lining. The coloring is unavoidable for anyone who regularly chews the preparation.*

CHICKEN KARAHI

This dish originates in North-West Frontier Province, where it is also known as *Balti Gosht* (Baal-TEE Gosht). It is fairly quick and simple to make and also popular in the rest of Pakistan. Karahi, which means wok in Hindi, can also be made with mutton. Simply substitute mutton on the bone for the chicken and cook it longer, until it becomes tender, before adding the tomatoes.

2 pounds (1 kg) chicken meat on the bone
2 teaspoons crushed garlic
4 tablespoons cooking oil
$\frac{1}{2}$ cup water
Salt to taste
Freshly ground black pepper
1 teaspoon red chili powder

5–6 medium-sized tomatoes (peeled and chopped)
A square inch of fresh ginger (peeled and julienned)
3–4 whole green chilies
2 tablespoons of fresh, chopped coriander leaves

Put the chicken and crushed garlic in a pan or wok with oil. Cover the pan and let the chicken cook on medium heat. Add $\frac{1}{2}$ cup water, and let the chicken cook until tender. When the meat has softened add the oil, salt, black pepper, and red chili powder. Increase the heat to evaporate the water, and then add the tomatoes, ginger, and green chilies. Lower the heat and cook with the pan covered for 5 to 10 minutes. When the tomatoes are soft, increase the heat and cook until the sauce thickens and clings to the meat. Add the coriander leaves, cover the pan, and turn off the heat. Serve with pita bread or plain boiled rice.

GULAB JAMUN

1 cup sugar
2 cups water
2–3 cardamom pods
1 cup powdered milk
1 tablespoon plain flour
1 tablespoon cooking oil
1 teaspoon baking powder
1 egg
Oil for deep-frying

In a pan, dissolve the sugar in the water, add the cardamoms, and bring the mixture to a boil. Let it boil for 15 minutes before taking it off the heat.

Mix the powdered milk, flour, oil, baking powder, and egg in a bowl. Knead the mixture until it turns into a soft dough. Make *jamun*, or small balls the size of large marbles, with the dough.

Heat the oil for deep frying the balls in a pan or wok. Test the oil temperature by dropping a ball into the heated oil and moving it around with a slotted spoon. If the ball does not rise to the top of the oil, it means that the oil is not hot enough. Wait for the oil to heat up a little more. If the ball immediately floats to the top of the oil and starts turning brown, turn down the heat and wait for the oil to cool slightly. At the right temperature the ball slowly rises to the top of the pan with the touch of a spoon. Gently press the balls with a slotted spoon until they turn light golden brown.

While frying the balls, heat the sugar syrup. Use the slotted spoon to remove the balls, and drain them on a kitchen towel before adding them to the sugar syrup. Put the balls in the syrup on a high flame and boil for 10 minutes, then turn the flame down and simmer for another five minutes. Do not cover the pan. Turn off the heat and serve the *gulab jamun* warm after 20 minutes.

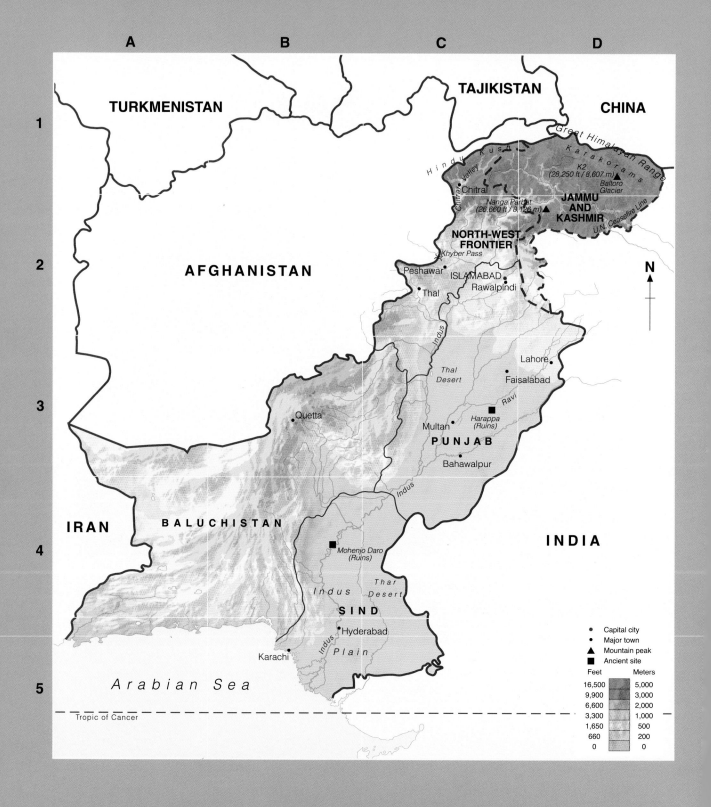

MAP OF PAKISTAN

ECONOMIC PAKISTAN

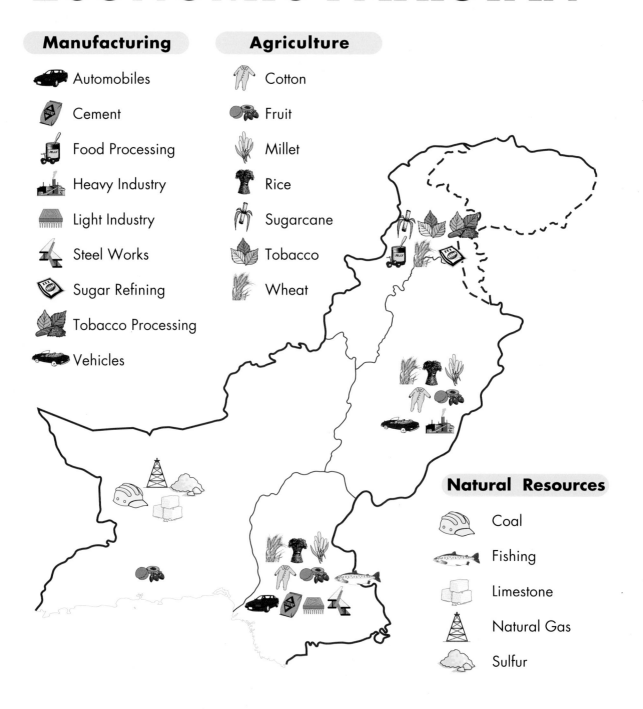

Manufacturing

- Automobiles
- Cement
- Food Processing
- Heavy Industry
- Light Industry
- Steel Works
- Sugar Refining
- Tobacco Processing
- Vehicles

Agriculture

- Cotton
- Fruit
- Millet
- Rice
- Sugarcane
- Tobacco
- Wheat

Natural Resources

- Coal
- Fishing
- Limestone
- Natural Gas
- Sulfur

ABOUT THE ECONOMY

GDP
$295.3 billion (2002)

GDP SECTORS
Agriculture 24 percent, industry 25 percent, services 51 percent (2002)

LAND AREA
310,402 square miles (803,940 sq km)

LAND USE
Arable land: 27.81 percent
Permanent crops: 0.79 percent
Other: 71.4 percent (1998)

AGRICULTURAL PRODUCTS
Cotton, wheat, rice, sugarcane, fruit, vegetables, dairy products, beef, mutton, poultry

INDUSTRIES
Textiles and apparel, food processing, beverages, construction materials, paper products, fertilizer, shrimp

CURRENCY
1 Pakistani rupee (PKR) = 100 paisas
USD1 = PKR57.33 (January 2004)
Notes: 5, 10, 50, 100, 500, 1000 rupees
Coins: 5, 10, 25, 50 paisas; 1 and 2 rupees

LABOR FORCE
40.4 million (2000)

UNEMPLOYMENT RATE
7.8 percent (2002)

INFLATION RATE
3.9 percent (2002)

MAJOR TRADE PARTNERS
Germany, Hong Kong, Japan, Saudi Arabia, United States, United Kingdom, United Arab Emirates

MAJOR EXPORTS
Textiles, rice, leather, sporting goods, carpets, rugs

MAJOR IMPORTS
Petroleum, petroleum products, machinery, chemicals, transportation equipment, edible oils, pulses, iron, steel, tea

PORTS AND HARBORS
Karachi, Port Muhammad Bin Qasim

AIRPORTS
124; 87 with paved runways

MAIN LINE TELEPHONES
3 million (1999)

INTERNATIONAL PARTICIPATION
United Nations (UN), South Asian Association for Regional Cooperation (SAARC), International Monetary Fund (IMF)

CULTURAL PAKISTAN

Shandur Pass Polo
Each year the Shandur Pass, located 12,205 feet (3,720 m) above sea level between Chitral and Gilgit, is the location for one of the most spectacular polo events in the world. This is arguably the highest site for any sports event. Teams from Chitral and Gilgit compete in the three-day festival.

Karakoram Highway
The Karakoram Highway is the highest road in the world, and snakes through some of the most spectacular and treacherous terrain. Built jointly by Pakistan and China, the highway took about 20 years to complete. At one point 25,000 people were employed to build the road, and it claimed more than 800 lives. The Khunjerab Pass (15,529 feet or 4,733 m above sea level) on the road is thought to be the highest paved-road international border crossing in the world.

Kalash Valley
The Kalash Valley in Chitral is home to the non-Muslim tribes of the Kalash who have a distinct but endangered lifestyle. There are conflicting theories about their origin, including one that claims the tribes are descended from Alexander the Great or his troops, who invaded the region in 326 B.C.

Taxila
Taxila, originally known as Takshasila, was the capital of the rich Gandhara Buddhist civilization, which flourished between 600 B.C. to 500 A.D. Visitors to this ancient city in Punjab can visit stupas, temples, monasteries, and ruins. The Taxila Museum is a rich storehouse of Gandhara sculpture and art.

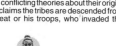

Shine of Shah Rukn-e-Alam
This shrine in Multan, Punjab, was built in the 14th century and is dedicated to the grandson of Bahauddin Zakaria, a famous Sufi saint. The octagonal shrine is topped by a dome, which is said to be the second largest in the world. This stunning building has won international awards for architecture.

K2
K2 is located on the Pakistan-China border. It rises to 28,251 feet (8,611 m) and is the second-highest mountain in the world. For a long time the mountain was considered impossible to climb until the first successful conquest in 1954. The icy peak is surrounded by six steep ridges and cannot be seen from any inhabited area.

Lahore Fort
The Lahore Fort is one of the three great forts built by the Mughals. Located in Lahore, which is the cultural capital of Pakistan, the fort was begun by Mughal emperor Akbar in the 16th century with later additions by his descendants Jahangir, Shah Jehan, and Aurangzeb. The fort is filled with opulent rooms, halls, and gardens.

Mohenjo Daro
Mohenjo Daro was first excavated in 1922 and is one of the most impressive archaeological sites in the world. Experts date the city to before 2500 B.C. Excavations indicate that a peaceful people once lived a high quality of life here, comparable to the great ancient civilizations of Mesopotamia and Egypt.

Makli Hills
Makli Hills, which is near Thatta in Sindh, is said to be the world's largest necropolis and is spread over an area of 3.9 square miles (10 sq km). It has a million medieval graves dating from the 12th to 18th centuries, which are carved with exquisite designs on stone and decorated with glazed tiles.

Shrine of Bhit Shah
This is the shrine of the great poet and Sufi saint Shah Abdul Latif, who died in 1752. During the festival held in his memory each year, thousands of devotees arrive at his shrine in Hyderabad to listen to songs and poems written by him.

ABOUT THE CULTURE

OFFICIAL NAME
Islamic Republic of Pakistan

NATIONAL FLAG
A green background with a white crescent and star represents the Muslim majority, while a vertical white band on the hoist side represents minorities.

NATIONAL ANTHEM
Pak Sarzameen Shad Bad, or Blessed Be the Sacred Land. Lyrics by Hafeez Jallundhari.

CAPITAL
Islamabad

OTHER MAJOR CITIES
Karachi, Lahore, Peshawar, Quetta, Rawalpindi

POPULATION
151 million (2003)

LIFE EXPECTANCY
Average—62.2 years
Men—61.3 years; women—63.1 years (2003)

MAJOR ETHNIC GROUPS
Punjabi, Sindhi, Pathan, Baloch, Muhajir

RELIGIOUS GROUPS
Muslims 97 percent (Sunni 77 percent, Shia 20 percent); Christians, Hindus, and others 3 percent

OFFICIAL LANGUAGE
Urdu

LITERACY RATE
45.7 percent

INTERNET USERS
1.2 million (2000)

IMPORTANT ANNIVERSARIES
Independence Day (Aug. 14), Pakistan Day (Mar. 23), Jinnah's Birthday (Dec. 25)

LEADERS IN POLITICS
Muhammad Ali Jinnah—Founding father of Pakistan
Zulfikar Ali Bhutto—First elected prime minister
Benazir Bhutto—First woman prime minister
Nawaz Sharif—Prime minister who decided Pakistan should conduct nuclear tests in response to those done by India
Mir Zafarullah Khan Jamali—Prime minister (2002)

FAMOUS PAKISTANIS
Nusrat Fateh Ali Khan (musician), Bapsi Sidhwa (writer), Sadequain (painter, calligrapher, and poet), Allama Iqbal (national poet), Faiz Ahmad Faiz (poet), Taufiq Rafat (poet), Imran Khan (cricketer and politician), Jahangir Khan and Jansher Khan (world squash champions), Dr. Abdus Salam (Nobel Laureate in Physics)

TIME LINE

IN PAKISTAN	IN THE WORLD
2500 B.C. Indus Civilization at its peak in the twin cities of Mohenjo-Daro and Harappa	
	753 B.C. Rome is founded.
	116–17 B.C. The Roman Empire reaches its greatest extent, under Emperor Trajan (98–17).
	A.D. 600 Height of Mayan civilization
A.D. 711 Muhammad bin Qasim, a 17-year-old general, comes to Sind and introduces Islam.	**1000** The Chinese perfect gunpowder and begin to use it in warfare.
1526 Mughal dynasty founder Babur establishes his empire across the Delhi Sultanate.	**1530** Beginning of trans-Atlantic slave trade organized by the Portuguese in Africa.
	1558–1603 Reign of Elizabeth I of England
	1620 Pilgrims sail the *Mayflower* to America.
	1776 U.S. Declaration of Independence
1858 The British announce the abolition of Mughal rule over India.	**1789–1799** The French Revolution
	1861 The U.S. Civil War begins.
	1869 The Suez Canal is opened.
1906 All-India Muslim League founded.	**1914** World War I begins.
1930 Dr. Muhammad Iqbal proposes the creation of an independent Islamic state in northwestern India (now Pakistan).	**1939** World War II begins.
1947 Partition of Indian subcontinent. The Islamic Republic of Pakistan is formed. War with India over the disputed territory of Kashmir.	**1945** The United States drops atomic bombs on Hiroshima and Nagasaki.

IN PAKISTAN	IN THE WORLD
1948 Muhammad Ali Jinnah dies.	
	1949 The North Atlantic Treaty Organization (NATO) is formed.
1951 Pakistan's first prime minister Liaquat Ali Khan is assassinated.	
	1957 The Russians launch Sputnik.
1965 War with India over Kashmir	
	1966–1969 The Chinese Cultural Revolution
1971 Civil war in Pakistan; the eastern section breaks away to become Bangladesh.	
1973 Zulfiqar Ali Bhutto becomes the first elected prime minister of Pakistan.	
1978 General Zia ul-Haq becomes president.	
1979 Soviet invasion of neighboring Afghanistan brings Afghan refugees into Pakistan.	
	1986 Nuclear power disaster at Chernobyl in Ukraine
1988 General Zia dies in a plane crash. Benazir Bhutto's party wins election.	
1990 Benazir Bhutto dismissed on corruption charges. Nawaz Sharif elected prime minister.	**1991** Break-up of the Soviet Union
1993 President Ghulam Ishaq Khan and Sharif resign. Benazir Bhutto is reelected.	
1997 Sharif wins the premiership.	**1997** Hong Kong is returned to China.
1998 Pakistan conducts nuclear tests.	
1999 Sharif is overthrown by General Pervez Musharraf, who declares himself president.	**2001** Terrorists crash planes in New York, Washington, D.C., and Pennsylvania.
2002 Musharraf wins five years in office. Mir Zafarullah Jamali becomes prime minister.	
	2003 War in Iraq

GLOSSARY

Ashura (AH-shoo-rah)
The 10th day of the first month of the Muslim calendar. On this day, Muslims commemorate the death of Hussein, Prophet Muhammad's grandson.

Azan (ah-ZAHN)
The Muslim call to prayer, which is an announcement of the first Pillar of Faith.

burqa (boor-KAH)
The robe and veil worn by traditional Muslim women that completely covers the body.

dupatta (doo-PAHT-tah)
Long, narrow scarf worn with *salwar kamiz*.

Haj (HAHJ)
Pilgrimage to Mecca, the spiritual center of Islam; a requirement for every Muslim and one of the five Pillars of Faith.

imam
Attendant of a mosque and prayer leader.

jirga (jerh-GAH)
Pashtun equivalent of a local council or parliament.

karez (kah-REZ)
Irrigation system in Baluchistan where water is channeled into underground tunnels and then drawn off into wells.

masjid (MAHS-jid)
Arabic and Urdu word for mosque.

melmastia (mel-MAHS-tyah)
The Pashtun concept of hospitality and protection for guests.

Muhajir (moo-HAH-jir)
The name given to most Muslims who arrived in Pakistan at the time of partition from India in 1947.

mullah (MOO-lah)
A cleric who is a scholar of Islamic law.

Pukhtunwali (PUHK-tuhn-wah-lee)
The Pashtun concept of honor by which they identify themselves.

purdah (POOR-dah)
The custom, found in certain traditional Muslim communities, of keeping women in seclusion. Women in *purdah* wear the *burqa* in public.

Ramadan (rah-mah-DAHN)
The ninth month of the Muslim calendar, during which the faithful fast from sunrise to sunset.

salwar kamiz (sahl-WAHR kah-MEEZ)
Long shirt and wide trousers forming the traditional dress of the Punjabis.

tandoor (TAHN-door)
Special oven for baking *naan*.

urs (OORS)
Saints' death anniversary, when their communion with God is celebrated.

FURTHER INFORMATION

BOOKS

Ahmad, Aisha, and Roger Boase. *Pashtun Tales From the Pakistan-Afghan Frontier.* London: Saqi Books, 2003.

Bajwa, Farooq. *Pakistan: A Historical and Contemporary Look.* New York: Oxford University Press, 1999.

Camerapix (Editor). *Spectrum Guide to Pakistan.* (1st American ed.) Northampton, MA: Interlink Publishing Group, 1998.

Insight Guides, Tony Halliday and Tahir Ikram. *Insight Guide Pakistan.* (Updated ed.) London: APA Productions, 1998.

Jones, Owen Bennett. *Pakistan: The Eye of the Storm.* (2nd ed.) New Haven, CT: Yale University Press, 2002.

Khan, Eaniqa and Rob Unwin. *Pakistan* (Country Insights). Texas: Raintree/Steck Vaughn, 1998.

Khan, Fazle Karim. *Geography of Pakistan—Environment, People, and Economy.* Karachi, Pakistan: Oxford University Press Pakistan, 1992.

Khan, Imran and Mike Goldwater. *Indus Journey: A Personal View of Pakistan.* London: Chatto & Windus, 1991.

King, John, Bradley Mayhew, and David St. Vincent. *Lonely Planet Pakistan.* (5th ed.) Footscray, Australia: Lonely Planet, 1998.

Mock, John and Kimberley O'Neil. *Trekking in the Karakoram and Hindukush* (2nd ed.) Footscray, Australia: Lonely Planet, 2002.

Shaw, Isobel. *Pakistan Handbook.* (2nd ed.) Chicago: Avalon Travel Publications, 1998.

Talbot, Ian. *Pakistan: A Modern History.* Hampshire, England: Palgrave Macmillan, 1999.

Winter, Dave and Ivan Mannheim. *Footprint Pakistan Handbook: The Travel Guide.* (2nd ed.) Bath, England: Footprint Handbooks, 1999

WEBSITES

Country study and guide to Pakistan. http://reference.allrefer.com/country-guide-study/pakistan/pakistan10.html

Tourism and travel guide to Pakistan. www28.brinkster.com/pakistan4ever/default.asp

Cultural attractions in Pakistan. www.khamisani.com/info.htm

Travel guide to Pakistan. www.lonelyplanet.com/destinations/indian_subcontinent/pakistan/

Central Intelligence Agency World Factbook webpage on Pakistan. www.odci.gov/cia/publications/factbook/geos/pk.html

Pakistan Tourism Development Corporation website. www.tourism.gov.pk

Urban Resource Center website for Karachi. www.urckarachi.org

VIDEOS

Nusrat! Live at Meany. Arab Film Distribution, 1999.

BIBLIOGRAPHY

Akhund, Nelma and Zainab Qureshi. *You Can Make a Difference: Environmental Public Interest Cases in Pakistan*. Karachi, Pakistan: Hamdard Press, 1998.

Amin, Mohamed. *Journey Through Pakistan*. Edison, New Jersey: Hunter Publishing, Inc., 1992.

Hughes, Libby. *Benazir Bhutto: From Prison to Prime Minister*. Minneapolis, Minnesota: Dillon Press, 1990.

Hussain, Jane. *An Illustrated History of Pakistan*. New York: Oxford University Press, 1998.

Khan, Fazle Karim. *The New Oxford Atlas for Pakistan*. Karachi: Oxford University Press Pakistan, 1991.

Pakistan in Pictures. Minneapolis, Minnesota: Department of Geography, Lerner Publications, 1994.

Winter, Dave and Ivan Mannheim. *Footprint Pakistan Handbook: The Travel Guide*. (2nd ed.) Bath, England: Footprint Handbooks, 1999.

The World Bank in Pakistan. http://lnweb18.worldbank.org/sar/sa.nsf/pakistan?OpenNavigator

Timeline of events in Pakistan's history. http://news.bbc.co.uk/1/hi/world/south_asia/1156716.stm

INDEX

real estate, 39
recycling, 46, 47
rickshaw production, 36
steelworks, 36
textiles, 36

Jinnah, Fatimah, 61
Jinnah, Muhammad Ali, 22, 23, 61, 119

Khan, Genghis, 21
Khan, Hashim, 106
Khan, Imran, 54, 108, 109
Khan, Ishaq, 29
Khan, Jahangir, 54
Khan, Jansher, 54
Khan, Nusrat Fateh Ali, 103
Khan, Yahya, 24
Khattak, Khushal Khan, 68
Khawak Pass, 20
Khyber Pass, 8, 22, 23, 54
Kurta Hizar, 53

Lahore Fort, 17, 21, 98, 99
languages, 8, 21, 23, 49, 51, 55, 82, 85, 86,
    87, 88, 89, 90, 91, 94, 102, 130
    Arabic, 8, 82, 86, 87, 89, 94
    English, 85
    Hindi, 87, 130
    Pashto, 90
    Persian, 21, 86, 87, 94, 102
    Punjabi, 85, 88, 89, 102
        Lahnda, 88
    Sanskrit, 87
    Sindhi, 85, 89
    Turkish, 87
    Urdu, 23, 51, 85, 86, 87, 88, 89, 94,
        102
Latif, Nargis, 47

Middle East, 7, 19, 20, 28, 37, 42, 46, 52,
    54, 56, 71, 73, 74, 75, 76, 77, 82, 93,
    94, 95, 96, 123
    Iran/Persia, 7, 20, 56, 71, 96, 123
    Iraq, 94
        Babylon, 20, 46
        Mesopotamia, 19
    Israel, 54, 56
    Saudi Arabia, 19, 28, 82
        Mecca, 73, 74, 75, 76, 77, 82
        Medina, 73, 74
    Syria, 94
    United Arab Emirates, 29, 43

minerals, 34, 35, 44, 46
    coal, 34, 35
    limestone, 34
    natural gas, 34, 35, 46
    oil, 44
    sulfur, 34
Mohammad, Hanif, 109
mountains, 8, 9, 11, 12, 13, 18, 20, 41, 55,
    107
    Baltoro Glacier, 9
    Godwin Austen, 9
    Hindu Kush, 8, 20, 55
    Himalayas, 8, 11, 18, 107
    K2, 9
    Karakoram Range, 8, 9
    Mount Everest, 9
Musharraf, General Pervez, 25, 27, 28,
    51, 83

oceans, 7, 11, 13, 15, 18, 36, 56
    Arabian Sea, 7, 11, 13, 15, 18, 36
    Caspian Sea, 56

Pakistan Muslim League, 27
Pakistan People's Party, 27
Partition, 17, 23, 51, 73, 75, 89, 119
provinces, 7, 8, 10, 11, 12, 13, 14, 18, 22,
    23, 27, 30, 33, 34, 35, 37, 42, 43, 44,
    50, 51, 52, 53, 54, 56, 60, 74, 83, 85,
    88, 89, 98, 100, 105, 108, 115, 120
    Baluchistan, 7, 8, 12, 13, 22, 23, 27,
        33, 34, 42, 43, 54, 56
    Jammu and Kashmir, 8, 30, 37, 83,
        108
    North-West Frontier, 7, 14, 22, 23, 27,
        33, 35, 54, 60
    Punjab, 7, 10, 11, 13, 18, 22, 23, 27,
        34, 35, 42, 43, 56, 83, 88, 98, 100,
        105, 115
    Sind, 7, 10, 11, 13, 22, 27, 35, 42, 44,
        50, 51, 52, 53, 56, 74, 85, 89, 98,
        120
Punjab Muslim League, 23
religions, 20, 22, 23, 25, 28, 29, 30, 31, 38,
    49, 51, 53, 55, 61, 63, 66, 70, 73, 74,
    75, 76, 77, 78, 79, 80, 81, 82, 83, 86,
    87, 88, 89, 93, 94, 98, 100, 101, 102,
    103, 110, 115, 116, 117, 118, 119, 120,
    125
    Buddhism, 93
    Christianity, 70, 74, 75, 81, 82, 83,
        102, 117

Jesuit, 102
Hinduism, 20, 22, 23, 30, 51, 53, 70,
    83, 86, 89, 120
Islam, 22, 23, 25, 28, 29, 30, 31, 38,
    49, 51, 55, 61, 66, 70, 73, 74, 75,
    76, 77, 79, 80, 81, 82, 86, 87, 93,
    94, 98, 100, 101, 102, 110, 116,
    117, 119, 120, 125
    Shiite, 80, 118
    Sufism, 79, 102, 103, 119, 120
    Sunni, 80, 118
Sikhism, 88

rivers, 7, 10, 11, 14, 15, 17, 18, 19, 20, 35,
    41, 50, 52
    Euphrates, 19
    Indus river, 7, 10, 11, 14, 17, 18, 20,
        35, 41, 52
    Nile, 11
    Tigris, 19
ruins, 17, 18, 93, 94, 95
    Harappa, 18, 93
    Mohenjo Daro, 17, 18, 19, 93, 94, 95
    Taxila, 93

shrines, 78, 79, 98, 102, 120
    Bhit Shah, 79, 98
    Lal Shahbaz Kalandar, 79, 120
    Rukh-e Alam 79
Sharif, Nawaz, 25, 27, 28, 29, 50
Soviet Union, 25, 30, 37, 90, 96
sports, 105, 106, 107, 108
    baseball, 108
    cricket, 106, 108
    field hockey, 106
    polo, 105, 107
    soccer, 106
    squash, 106
    tennis, 106
    volleyball, 106

Thar Desert, 14, 53, 74
Turkey, 52, 123

ul-Haq, General Muhammad Zia, 25, 27,
    38, 50, 61, 83, 109
United Kingdom, 23, 28, 35, 37, 71, 103,
    106, 107, 108
United Nations, 30
United States of America, 25, 28, 37, 41,
    53, 83, 106
urs, 78, 119, 120